W9-AAY-966

AN OLD-FASHIONED

Christmas

Sweet Traditions for Hearth and Home

ELLEN STIMSON

Photography by Natalie Stultz

Illustrations by Jonathan Weiss

The Countryman Press

A division of W. W. Norton & Company

Independent Publishers Since 1923

The Countryman Press
www.countrymanpress.com

A division of W. W. Norton & Company, Inc.,
500 Fifth Avenue, New York, NY 10110
www.wwnorton.com

For information about special discounts for bulk purchases, please contact
W. W. Norton Special Sales at specialsales@wwnorton.com or 800-233-4830

Printed in the United States of America

An Old-Fashioned Christmas
978-1-58157-328-2

10 9 8 7 6 5 3 4 3 2 1

For my Hannah,
because Christmas really is our legacy . . .

Contents

Prologue

The ornaments are the first things I would save in a fire.

Now, I am not just sure how I would manage to get them down from the attic fast enough. They're someplace behind all those out-of-season clothes, the kids' furniture that we're storing "just until I move to a bigger place, Mom," and all those piles that I Really Must Go Through . . . before I pitch them for good. Once I'm past all that, it would probably be a straight shot to the actual tubs filled with our most precious family keepsakes. But that is just a detail. Let us just hope it is a slow house fire. Because, those lopsided plastic bins are chock-full of our oldest and best memories. We are (possibly the truest thing about us, even) a Christmas family.

We are the kind of people who decide where the Christmas tree might go before we buy the house. (Doesn't everyone?) When we moved to Vermont, it was at least in part because it seemed to be the single Christmasiest state in the Union. With its trademark snow, piney forests, sleigh rides, and wood smoke curling out of village chimneys, Vermont was practically invented for the Christmas postcard. We've got your Christmas goose and the maple syrup glaze you will use to baste it. We even have moose wandering around the mountains and drinking out of the rivers. They are a really good double for reindeer in a holiday pinch.

Winter is long in the North Country. The lights and sounds of Christmas get my people through.

Many years ago, when the children were young, our family began an annual tradition we call Christmas Adventure. We go away the first weekend in December. It's how we kick off Christmas. We eat a fancy supper out and stay in a hotel or a cozy B&B. We wander around looking at Christmas decorations, listening to carols, and generally getting in the holly jolly mood. There is little variety from year to year, and that is just how we like it. Oh, some years we may see a holiday movie, and others we might go skating. But every year, every single year for the last twenty-eight, we all go shopping for one new ornament each. It is a ritual without compare.

My husband, John, chooses silly snowmen and penguins most years. He's the quiet one, and there is an irony about his choice. Hannah prefers to stay within the animal kingdom. Dolphins, elephants, raccoons. Eli is reliable, too. He likes big, elaborate, spun-glass concoctions that fairly scream, "I AM an Ornament!" Benjamin's choices follow his current passions. That

might be fishing or soccer. I tend to go in for home and hearth and Santa.

Eventually, we come back home and cut down the tree. John always thinks the tree is too big. I always fret that it's too small. Most years, we are both wrong. We wrestle it into the house, put it up to decorate, and then, one by one, all of those beautiful fragile ornaments collected lovingly through the years come out of their tissue paper, taking their places once more. Back where they belong.

Once the tree is decorated, it isn't long until the first Slovak nut roll comes out of the oven. We bake all of John's grandmother's favorite recipes. These recipes were her mother's, and they've been handed down through five gen-

erations. Our Hannah makes them now. There will also be 1970s icebox cakes from my mom's recipe file. And my own rich winey stews and yeasty breads that can hold a body over till the thaw.

Lots of American families, religious or not, have their own Christmas stories. I always loved listening to the women at our local beauty shop when I was a little girl. Mom was of a generation of women who were at the beauty shop every week, come snow or shine. Well, especially come snow. That sorority of women would gather together and pass the time under the dryer with stories. They would tell about the Christmas that got away, the time the tree fell over, or, best of all, the Christmas when everything just worked. There was a storytelling tradition among those women, who, after all, were mostly the keepers of Christmas. They were the ones who shopped and baked, wrapped and decorated. They did it all as a giant gesture of love in hopes that they were forging memories that would last forever. Christmas was their legacy. Sometimes the memories were not the ones they planned to make. But sometimes those perfect holidays that they longed for actually came true. They would share stories and recipes with one another and with daughters-in-law, nieces, and neighbors. In this way, the traditions got handed down and fluffed up. The torches got passed.

Every family has a Christmas story. These are a few of ours.

Saint Louie Nick

Christmas is romantic. You've got wood smoke and warm woolen blankets. There will be snow and bells. Cinnamon and nutmeg; butter and sugar. It even comes with its own soundtrack. It's the best time to fall in love.

I was beyond smitten.

He liked quirky indie movies, read lots of great books, listened to Ella and Van, and knew how to cook. He even wrote actual poetry. And he could kiss. That just about summed up my wish list at the time. So when my now-husband and I started to get serious, and it was December, it felt like a sign. I was a Christmas girl, so it was time to find out if we really were made for one another. Then out of nowhere he sent me a Christmas card signed, *Merry Xmas, John.*

It was not an auspicious Christmas beginning, as beginnings go. So I sent it right back with a note that said, *I really think you could do better. Love, Ellen.*

I was cheeky.

It turned out he could do better.

I got a new card two days later.

That card was signed, *I will always remember this Christmas and how wonderful you are. Love, John.*

That really was better. Way better. I was in.

Our first pre-Christmas Adventure was at a little inn in Elsah, Illinois. Perched on the bluffs over the Missouri River, Elsah is the one tiny little town in the Midwest that most resembles New England. I had always fantasized about living in Vermont, and this was as close as I was getting at that time.

We had a Saturday-afternoon lunch at the Broadway Oyster Bar in St. Louis, listening to jazz. We wandered around town in a snow flurry looking at all the downtown holiday window decorations, especially the ornaments.

That was when we saw him. The ornament was a little resin Santa that looked like he was blastin' old Cole Porter tunes on his saxophone. He was hanging out on a tree at the florist shop. We ran in and bought him in a cloud of giggly agreement seconds later.

Our first ornament.

We still had to get John his first tree, but by the time he was holding that Santa in his hand and kissing me, the rest of this story was only a matter of time. It all came true. Every single bit.

Chapter One

Vermonters

Winter settles in and simplifies everything. The essentials of life in Vermont are heat, food, shelter, and plumbing. The rest is just for show. The life that you talk about on Facebook is mostly fiction. When it's fifteen below, temperature is practically all you ever think about. A quiet heat source would be nice, but in an 1838 farmhouse it isn't essential, so long as you are warm. Real life is the reassuring sound of the old boiler chugging back to life every morning. Real life is the smell of a steamy cassoulet simmering on the stove.

In winter, there is this quiet gray light, with snow falling most days. The flakes blow through the branches, leaving behind a shiny trail. The fires are burning and the light from our windows casts a sweet glow on the picket fence, which is just another shade of white in a whole landscape of white. There are the skeletons of the trees. Bare bones. The blurry outline of the chicken house shines with the weird red heat-lamp light that we have come to think of as the Bethlehem light—seen from afar, always burning, ever warm. The boiler comes on in the morning with a racket, but thankfully, it comes on.

We have made some trade-offs up here in the North Country for the right to see these mountains every day, to breathe this good air, and to live this life beside the waterfalls, up close to the coyotes and the bears. We may not have as many restaurants and cinemas or shiny shoes and fancy hair salons as you'll find in the big city, but what we do have are these magnificent views, the smell of wood smoke in the air, and the quiet satisfaction of a life lived on its own terms.

Recently, newscasters in these parts have started talking about arctic winds and something called the polar vortex. That term may have been new to me, but the deep meaning

of winter surely isn't. Winter is a good time to lean in to the weather and the landscape. The woodland animals hibernate and we have time for deeper reflection and quieter pursuits. Vermonters, and especially the women of Vermont, have a long tradition of bringing the natural world inside, and the kind of long, slow cooking that warms and brings real, sustaining comfort.

This was not always the story of our lives. For our first forty years John and I were Midwesterners. We both grew up in a little steel town just east of the Mississippi, not far from St. Louis. Later, we lived in St. Louis proper; it was only in 2003 that we packed up our family and headed to a place where winter is a serious business. Sure, we had snow in St. Louis, just not much of it. And almost never at Christmas. For a girl who had always loved Christmas, New England was like a dream come true.

When I first got here, I took pictures everywhere I went. I was constantly sharing scenes with my friends back home. There were trees that looked like the elves had dipped them in sparkly snow, there were romantic sleigh rides, and there were kids with colorful hats and mittens, laughing on old-fashioned sleds. I have a Facebook friend in sunny California who, after looking at a few . . . I don't know, thousand or so . . . of these postcard shots, sweetly (?) suggested that I get some cats and name them Currier and Ives.

Of course, I never took pictures of the salt stuck between the floorboards in the kitchen, or the pile of lip balm and Kleenex we kept by the back door so that anyone venturing out in the twenty-below weather would have decent accoutrements. That part was true, but not much worth telling.

Winter always gets rolling with the Christmas preparations. I don't really know how you could stand the long winters up here if you don't ski or have your own special way of digging in and celebrating the season. For me, it is all about the food and the holidays. November would be unbearably bleak if not for Thanksgiving. By the end of October, the leaves have all fallen off the trees and blown away. There is a letdown in November after the riotous party colors are gone. The days are chilly and gray. There is hardly ever any snow to lighten the landscape, and the days are short. Even the sun is depressed in November.

So I plan for the feast. I spend Saturday afternoons in front of a fire, reading my old cookbooks and sending lists of possible menus to our guests. These food letters are mostly just a silly game, since no matter what cool culinary ideas I conjure up, everyone wants the same old standards every year. Every. Single. Time.

We welcome folks in and celebrate with food, board games, and laughter. We take the "thankful" part of Thanksgiving seriously. Each year, we go around the table—or nowadays pull up Skype for at least one far-flung family member—and we list out those things we were thankful for in the past year. Sometimes it's sincere. Sometimes it's a little silly. But we're always thankful. And stuffed. Those recipes everyone wants at Thanksgiving are a long way from light. Still, eventually we get through November, and then *bam!* it's December again and the celebrating gets serious.

The first thing we do to get ready is decorate the house. In my old city life, the decorating involved many trips to the florist. We moved to Vermont in the month of June, and by winter I had already established a relationship with my local nursery, Mettowee Mill. They'd had lots of gorgeous hydrangeas that had already made their way into my yard over the summer. So when it came time to fill the vases with winter greenery and red berries, I headed right over.

It was early December and it was cold. On the way to the nursery, I passed a wooded hillside covered with winterberries. I imagined bunches of them in vases on the mantel and hoped they'd have some at the nursery. I considered getting out and snipping a tiny branch to show the folks at Mettowee, you know, as an example of what I was thinking. But it was awfully cold, there was already a lot of snow, and my footwear was not up to a hillside ramble.

When I got to the nursery, I tried to explain that I was looking for winterberries, maybe some juniper and holly would be good, too. I was chattering away to Robin, a real Vermonter, who had seemed a bit surprised to see me.

I kept talking. "On the way here I saw these gorgeous berries by the side of the road. I would have picked a little to show you, but, well . . . I'm not wearing the right kind of shoes. Dumb, huh? So, do you know the ones I mean?"

Vermonters are careful communicators. They take their time. But when they speak they are nothing if not clear.

"You want to show us where you saw them?"

"Oh, sure. That's great. You wanna ride in my car?" I would just run her down to the spot where I'd seen them, and once she identified them I'd bet she'd have a good supplier. I wondered how long it would take for them to arrive.

But Robin wasn't finished. "We can go cut them and bring them back here," she said. "I'd be glad to sell them to you."

"Great! It'll just take a . . . wait . . . er . . . cut them and sell them to me?"

She was kidding, right? "You guys don't actually cut them from the side of the road?" I mean, I'm all for local sourcing, but that seemed odd.

"No." She smiled. "But that's where I cut mine. And if you want to buy some, that's where I'd get yours, too."

Cut. Mine.

She was still smiling. It was a kindly smile.

In retrospect, it could have been much worse.

I think I understood. Or at least almost understood. This is Vermont. I'd moved up here to be closer to the natural world. And here it was. I lived surrounded by the woods now. There was an actual mountain right behind my house. Or a high green hill, anyway. Okay, it's a knoll, but still . . . mountain-ish. In St. Louis, I racked up a bill with a florist to get the house looking just right. But here? Here, I could cut all the red-and-green stuff I wanted to from the side of the road and decorate my house with it!

It was a revelation.

I smiled right back. I got it. It might have taken me a while, but now I understood. I was going to go home, put on my boots, grab my dogs and some loppers. We'd walk through the woods and cut beautiful stuff for my winter decorations.

And that's just what I did later that afternoon. There was a nor'easter headed our way and I wanted to get some color inside before it showed up. The days had been a run of drab pewter since about mid-November. It was a lot like living inside an Ansel Adams gallery. Only colder. The dark comes early and the temperatures dip even faster. The veil is thinner this time of year. We notice and feel things that the color and noise of spring and summer cover up. There is a reason big feelings get described as raw just like this December weather does. There is a wistfulness that seems to settle in around November, and it stays till the holidays take over.

But the celebrations were near. I was, by golly, going to make us a Mountain Christmas. The dogs ran ahead while I cut holly from my own bushes and picked up white birch and pinecones in the woods behind our house. I could fill our glass bowls with the pinecones. I might even paint their edges white so they looked snow-dipped. The white birch barks were hollow circles in the shapes of the logs they once wrapped. I imagined filling those with pine. Maybe I could cut little holes in the tops to let greenery peek through, and then scatter them on tables and sideboards. It was going to be gorgeous. There would be piney boughs draped everywhere, and winterberries—I found 'em!—and North Country juniper in all the vases. We would fight the darkness with little white fairy lights strung along every porch and balcony. It was my first Vermont winter, and I was ready with light and color.

Winter Suppers

A word about the recipes. These foods are my old friends. Like their human counterparts, they are deeply satisfying, easy, and generous. What they are not is entirely precise. You will not, for example, find much information about the right kind of pan to use for a particular dish here. I do have favorite pots and pans, of course. I have an old Griswold cast-iron pan of my grandmother's that is so well-seasoned it is like a slick of black ice. I love that pan. It has nestled so many knobs of butter and piles of garlic that it has a taste all its own. It would not be a good pan for sweet pancakes, but it is perfect for a pork chop. So I have plenty of favorite pans, but so do you. We should all use the ones we love best.

I am not someone who measures precisely. I am more of an estimator. When a recipe calls for a teaspoon of salt, I grab a big fat pinch and throw in a little extra for good measure. I have tried to give approximations of measurements here. But think of these recipes as a guide. More a campfire story than a deposition. Precision is not required. It is not even particularly welcome.

These are a homecook's recipes. A little less salt or a little more sugar won't hurt anything. Let your own preferences be your guide. If you like thyme better than tarragon, I might think you are crazy, but by all means make the substitution. Personally, I am the girl who subs in tarragon at every opportunity. You will not find directions about frothing the butter here or how many seconds to sauté those shallots, but you just might find something good to have for a wintry supper.

And a word about the meat seasonings: I like a steak-rub spice mix sold as Ranch Hands Hearty from Brockton Spice Company (see Appendix II, New England Flavors).

We call it Peltier's Rub at our house, 'cause we used to sell it at Peltier's (a quaint old country store featured in a little book called *Mud Season*, which everyone should Buy

And Read Right Now This Second!). I have bought Peltier's Rub by the fifteen-pound bag-
ful ever since. If you have your own favorite savory rub, by all means use that. Or make
your own with garlic and a mix of peppers and salts.

Braised Winter Short Ribs

This has become my favorite go-to winter supper. I made it up in a cold hotel bed one night when I was wishing for home. It was early December and I was in Boston on a business trip. There was an icy rain pelting the windows and my normally cozy hotel was suffering through a power outage. The generator was working only intermittently. I had asked for and gotten more blankets but I was still cold. So I snuggled under pillows and covers and began making up my menus. These short ribs with chocolate and chili were on the table the next weekend. We had a few fat snowflakes falling and a cheery little fire and I have been making them ever since. They make the kitchen smell warm and steamy. They have a deep, rich flavor that tastes like wintertime.

Serve with a good Cru Beaujolais for a soft, warm feeling of contentment that will get you through winter down to about minus-ten degrees. (After that, nothing much helps.)

INGREDIENTS

1   cup beef stock
⅓   cup good balsamic vinegar
½   cup dark cocoa powder
¼   cup brown sugar or honey
2 or 3 garlic cloves, minced
Red pepper flakes
Tarragon
1   bottle (ish) red wine
3   pounds boneless beef short ribs
A little bit of good olive oil

Combine beef stock, vinegar, cocoa powder, brown sugar, garlic, a dash of pepper flakes, tarragon (a lot, and fresh if you can get it), and wine and bring to a simmer.

Sear the ribs in a little olive oil on very high heat for a deep brown color, and then put ribs into liquid mix. Bring liquid to a boil, then reduce heat and simmer till ribs are tender . . . couple of hours, usually.

Serve atop Cheddar Grits (page 196) for a deeply rich and satisfying winter meal.

Coq au Vin

You eat this in a French bistro and it seems like maybe the chef brought his great grandfather's recipe with him and there is no way you will figure out the secret. Only, it turns out that heat and mushrooms and wine *are* the secret and you can make this just as well as he can. Sometimes I use sausage and sometimes pancetta. I might throw in some cognac for a husky caramel-at-the-end layer of flavor. This is a deeply resonant and beautiful dish. I like the surprise of serving it over a warm salad of winter greens so you get that tang of vinegar to offset the intense flavor of the stew.

INGREDIENTS

Roasting chicken

Olive oil

Steak seasoning

Butter for sautéing

2 onions, quartered and sliced

1½ cups shiitake mushrooms, sliced

⅓ cup dark cocoa powder

⅓ cup flour

1 bottle red wine

Balsamic vinegar

2 to 3 cloves garlic, chopped

Fresh tarragon, chopped

2 to 3 carrots, chopped

2 to 3 turnips, chopped

Cut up your chicken or have a butcher do it for you. Coat chicken pieces in olive oil and steak seasoning. Sear on all sides.

In a separate pan, melt a knob of butter and lightly sauté the onions. When onions are translucent, add to the chicken. In the pan you used for the onions, add another knob of butter and lightly sauté the mushrooms. Stir in the cocoa powder and add all to the chicken. Add flour and stir.

Add a bottle of good red table wine. (I like Evodia. Pour yourself a glass.) Add a drizzle of balsamic vinegar. Add the garlic and tarragon. Bring to a gentle boil, then turn heat down to low. Cover and cook, low and slow, for 90 minutes.

Add the carrots and turnips, then go on to cook an additional 2½ hours for 4 hours total, until the meat is just about falling off the bone. Serve atop wintery greens.

Winter Greens with Dried Cranberries and Warm Mustard Champagne Vinegar

The beauty shop ladies used to call these wilted salads. Most of theirs used bacon. I tarted this one up with the berries and champagne vinegar, but they were plenty good back in the day. They still are.

INGREDIENTS

1½ pounds fresh spinach

Butter, for sautéing

Mushrooms (I like shiitake. Use your favorite and slice them thickly according to their shape and size.)

1   red onion, thinly sliced

2   dashes nutmeg

1   cup dried cranberries

1   cup pecans

1   shallot, diced

½   cup Dijon mustard

3   tablespoons balsamic vinegar or champagne vinegar

1   tablespoon sugar

Sauté spinach in butter in batches as it cooks down.

In a separate pan, sauté mushrooms and red onions, then add to the spinach. Add nutmeg, cranberries, and pecans. Transfer to a serving dish.

In a separate pan, sauté shallot in butter. Add mustard, vinegar, and sugar. Drizzle over the greens.

I like to serve with Coq au Vin, or a good Parmesan pork chop.

Creamed Spinach

People want fancy sides during the holidays. I do not know why. There is nothing wrong with serving creamed spinach with just about anything. You can always get good spinach any time of year, for one thing. And everybody likes the taste, for another. If your family comes down with a winter cold over the holidays, cook them this. If you have the cold, use frozen spinach. It's just as good here and shortcuts are your friends, especially in December.

Also, this is the only time in my life I will ever say these next four words: Don't overdo the cream.

Wash and chop spinach, removing stems. Heat pan, melt butter, and then add a bit of olive oil. Mix in onions and garlic. Cook 2 minutes until soft. (Don't let the garlic burn!) Add spinach and cook about 2 minutes more. Add salt and pepper, nutmeg, and heavy cream. Mix well. Cook until liquid is reduced by half, 3 to 4 minutes. Serve hot.

INGREDIENTS

2   bunches fresh spinach
2   tablespoons butter
Olive oil
1   Vidalia onion, minced
1   clove of garlic, minced
Sea salt and fresh pepper
2   teaspoons nutmeg
¼   cup heavy cream

Guinness Beef Stew

Here's a hearty stew that you cannot mess up. Just cook it a long time with the lid slid off at a little slant to let the rich steam fill up your kitchen. Serve it with good crusty bread. Would it be too much goodness to bake the bread yourself? You will have the rich aroma of the stew and the baking bread in competition and your nose will not know which way to go. But it might be the happiest day you have spent alone ever. And by the time your hungry family shows back up from a day's skiing they will think you are a genius.

Mix meat pieces with a small amount of olive oil. Roll pieces in steak seasoning. To a heavy-bottomed stock pot warmed over medium-high heat, add oil and sear meat on all sides (warm pan, cold oil). Toward the end of the searing, add onions.

Reduce heat to medium, add flour, and coat beef and onion mixture. Add two cans of Guinness. Add tarragon, cocoa powder, garlic, caynne pepper, and cocoa chili seasoning, if using. Bring liquid to a gentle boil, then turn down the heat. Cover and cook, low and slow, stirring occasionally, for 1½ hours. Add more Guinness if you start to lose the liquid. (Sometimes I add a little tomato paste if I have it. Red wine will also work if you need to add more liquid.)

Add potatoes and cook for an additional 30 minutes. Add chopped carrots and cook a final 30 minutes. The entire cooking time should be near 3 hours, until the meat is falling apart and the sauce is thick and fragrant.

INGREDIENTS

3   pounds stewing beef (chuck or round), cut into 1½-inch cubes (If you're pressed for time, as I usually am, you can use strip steak, which cooks to tenderness faster. I have even been known to buy tenderloin in a real pinch right before company was coming.)

Olive oil for coating and searing beef

3 to 4 tablespoons steak seasoning

2   medium onions, roughly chopped

¼   cup flour

2   cans Guinness

Fresh tarragon and lots of it, chopped

½   cup cocoa powder

2   garlic cloves, finely chopped

1   dash cayenne pepper

2   dashes cocoa chili blend seasoning, optional

Half a small bag new potatoes or similar, cut in half

Carrots (as many as you'd like), chopped

Citrus Soy Pork Loin

Everybody serves ribs. People understand barbecue. But you can still surprise your guests with an interesting pork loin. Pork does not have to be cooked to within an inch of its life anymore, either: 145 degrees with a pink center is where you are aiming. This one is especially good in winter with the comfort of a tomato pie and a wonderful curried cauliflower (recipes follow).

INGREDIENTS

Salt and pepper to season

1- to 1½- pound pork loin

MARINADE

2   cups soy sauce

2   cups brown sugar

½   cup champagne vinegar

½   cup olive oil

Juice of 1 orange

1   shallot, minced

Handful of fresh tarragon

Season the meat with salt and pepper and let sit at room temperature. Mix together marinade ingredients, and combine marinade and pork loin in a resealable plastic bag. Marinate for at least one hour, turning bag occasionally so that all parts of loin soak in liquid.

Prepare a hot grill. Set loin on the grill and shoot for a nice sear. (If you don't have a grill you can do this right on the stove either on the griddle if you have one or in a really hot pan; cast-iron would be my first choice) Grill about 8 minutes on both sides until medium-rare. Use a meat thermometer to check for doneness. The ends will be more well-done than the center, for those who prefer that sort of thing.

Luxurious Garlicky Scalloped Potatoes

Rich, buttery, and lush. The word "luxurious" is not enough on its own to do this gratin justice. It is special enough to serve on Christmas Eve . . . the biggest night of the year. The person has not yet been born who won't enjoy these potatoes. Even the rice people will cross over when you put this on their plates. You can make them ahead and reheat them for your dinner party. They are great the next day, too.

INGREDIENTS

2½ pounds red potatoes

1½ cups half-and-half

3 cups heavy cream

¾ ounce minced fresh garlic

½ teaspoon salt

½ teaspoon ground white pepper

Butter for casserole dish

Preheat the oven to 400 degrees.

Wash and peel the potatoes. Slice potatoes ⅛- to ¼-inch thick. Combine potatoes, half-and-half, heavy cream, garlic, and salt and pepper in a saucepan over medium-high heat and bring to a boil. Reduce to a simmer and cook for 6 to 8 minutes.

Pour potatoes and sauce into a buttered casserole dish and bake for about 45 minutes.

Curried Cauliflower

I started messing around with cauliflower when I was still in high school. You could make a whole meal from one. Add cheese and it tasted almost like snack food. Add curry and you could imagine yourself living a more exotic life, one where you wore pink and orange scarves and jangly bracelets. This little number is a perfect backdrop to the pork.

Trim off leaves and cut out central core of cauliflower; break the head into florets, and peel and slice the core. Halve the florets lengthwise.

Bring ½ cup water to a boil in a 2-quart saucepan over medium heat, then add the cauliflower pieces and cook, covered, until tender, about 5 minutes.

Drain cauliflower and place pieces in a food processor. Add cream, butter, curry powder, salt, and pepper and purée to desired consistency, adding more liquid or more butter, if desired. (I like the consistency a bit rough, but you can purée for a smoother, more elegant dish.)

Check for seasonings and serve immediately, or turn purée out into a gratin dish and reheat in a 250-degree oven when ready to serve.

INGREDIENTS

- 1 medium head cauliflower
- ¼ cup heavy cream
- 2 tablespoons sweet butter, softened, plus more to taste
- 2 teaspoons curry powder
- ½ teaspoon salt
- ⅛ teaspoon ground white pepper

Tomato Pie

I make this with fresh tomatoes in the summer, but you can substitute canned tomatoes in the winter and the pie will still be delicious. Honest.

INGREDIENTS

2 cups flour

1 stick butter, cold and diced

4 teaspoons baking powder

¾ cup buttermilk

PIE FILLING

1½ cups grated sharp cheddar cheese, divided

2 (32 ounce) cans chopped tomatoes

1 handful of snipped chives, divided

Fresh basil, a handful, divided

⅓ cup lemon mayonnaise (You can buy this at the store or make your own by adding the juice of a whole lemon.)

Preheat oven to 400 degrees.

Combine flour, butter, baking powder, and buttermilk and mix gently until combined. The less time you spend handling it the better. When the dough is not too sticky, divide it in half. Line your pie plate with half of it and then add ¾ cup of the cheddar and layer tomatoes, chives, and basil on top of the cheese. Add the mayonnaise and another ¾ cup of the cheese on top of that. Scatter more chives and basil on top, then tear off pieces of the remaining dough and stretch them out on top, leaving little gaps of red in between. Bake for 25 or 30 minutes. The pie will look very Christmasy. The whole meal, as served with the pork and cauliflower, is quite satisfying and dear.

Roasted Balsamic Brussels Sprouts

When I was a little girl I hated this vegetable above all others. That was probably because they were always boiled in an open pot where they turned to mush and smelled up the whole kitchen along the way. It wasn't until I was in my forties that I finally tasted some prepared by a cook who understood what these babies could do.

When you clean them, save the little leaves that fall off the sprouts. They will get crispy in the oven and add a nice snappy crunch to the dish. You can't hurt these. You actually want to burn them a little. They are also delicious prepared without the pancetta, for the vegetarians in the group.

Preheat oven to 400 degrees.

Trim Brussels sprouts and cut them in half. Place Brussels sprouts in a bowl, including the loose leaves. Add pancetta, olive oil, and salt and pepper. Toss. Spread Brussels sprouts in a single layer on a cookie sheet.

Roast for 20 to 30 minutes until tender and lightly browned. Toss once or twice during roasting. Remove from the oven and drizzle with balsamic vinegar. Sprinkle with sea salt.

INGREDIENTS

1½ pounds Brussels sprouts

4 ounces pancetta, diced

¼ cup good peppery olive oil

Sea salt

Freshly ground black pepper

Balsamic vinegar (buy the best you can find)

Coffee-Encrusted Skirt Steak

Two things—I am a carnivore, and I love coffee beyond all reason. I sometimes crave leftover steak with a handful of sea salt for breakfast. There is always a mug of thick bitter coffee swirled with real cream alongside. But I am not someone blessed with patience. So flavorful skirt steak is fast and achievable for me. (The inside cut is the most flavorful—outside is always less beefy-tasting.) For a long time I relied on good balsamics and salt and not much else. Then one day, inevitably, I had the steak, company due in about an hour, but no balsamic to be found. What I did have were a bunch of those little single-serving espresso cups. I figured I could extract their coffee granules and make a rub. Wonder how that would taste? Turned out the answer was "fantastic," and I have been making it this way ever since. This one will not let you down and is interesting enough for any kind of company. Plus it smells divine.

INGREDIENTS

2   pounds inside skirt
     steak

Steak seasoning

Brown sugar

Ground coffee

Tarragon, optional, fresh if
     you have it

Olive oil

Liberally coat steak with steak seasoning and cover that with a thin layer of brown sugar, and then a layer of ground coffee on top of that, and then tarragon, if using. Just pat it on there. Then wrap the meat in plastic wrap (seal it tightly so no air gets in).

Let it sit in the dry rub for at least an hour in the refrigerator. When ready to cook, remove wrap and drizzle a little olive oil on the steak and place it on a hot grill (or under the broiler). Grill two minutes per side. Take it off and put it on a cool surface and let it rest for 5 minutes. Thinly slice it across the grain.

Serve atop Cheddar Grits (page 196).

Electric Beets

The beet has, like the Brussels sprout, been much maligned. Not these, though. These are dazzling. Hot pink. They are splashy on the plate and make any meal more festive. You can sprinkle some ground-up pistachios over the top if you want a little red and green both. Pistachios and beets are a nice textural and flavor blend too. I promise you these will make new beet converts right at your table.

Fill a pot with water and set it over high heat (make sure you have enough water to cover the beets at a boil).

Rinse beets and cut off tops and roots. Place beets in boiling water and boil until fork-tender. Drain beets and run them under cold water.

Peel beets with your hands under running cold water. Slice into ¼-inch-thick slices.

Dice bulbs and tops of green onions and gently sauté in olive oil for 3 to 4 minutes. Add beets to the pan, toss, and sauté until they are heated through. Add sour cream and mix until the entire dish is bright pink. Plate and finish with sea salt.

These will make a vibrant addition to your table.

INGREDIENTS

1   large bunch of beets
1   bunch green onions
Olive oil
1   tablespoon sour cream
Sea salt

The Dowry

My grandmother's Minnie Mouse ornament, along with Donald Duck, his duckling nephews, and a few others, decorated her little Christmas tree throughout my childhood. I inherited Minnie and one of Donald's family from her when I was about eighteen years old. Only Minnie survives. She lives tucked in a cotton nest in an old wooden box most of the year up in the attic, but when Christmas comes, she is back in her rightful place, the first ornament beneath our star.

Minnie Mouse reminds me of divinity candy so sweet it made your teeth hurt, and coffee-can transports with grass beds and holes in the lid that got frogs and other critters safely from Gram's house to mine. Grandma McIlvoy knew that most problems could be solved in long chats with her neighbor Lillian over the back fence. She also knew that a thick cup of hot chocolate could pretty well mend anything. I spent many Saturday mornings in her yard chasing frogs and butterflies. Everything lived in that wild overgrown space with snapdragons, cockscombs, and violets growing like crazy. I lived there, too. Anytime I need reminding, I have Minnie.

Chapter Two
The Beauty Shop

The baking gets started in earnest just after Thanksgiving. It doesn't let up around here till January, when the new bathroom scale starts its annual taunting. Ten pounds of butter, fifteen pounds of flour, seven pounds of sugar, eight bags of chocolate chips, and a bottle of good Madagascar Bourbon vanilla extract later, and *bam!* there you have your Christmas kitchen. Every year there are all kinds of cookies, of course, and piles of fudge sitting next to cakes, candy, and pie.

A word about pie. You can mend a broken heart in front of a fire with a really good piece of pie. My mother had a pie bakery in the basement of our house when I was growing up. And I had many a broken heart, so I have a lot of experience with pie as mender. As a result of many years of practice from the time the step stool got me high enough, I can roll out flaky pie dough with the best of them. You can celebrate any-

thing better with something sweet and gooey. Our holiday wouldn't be complete without platters of family Christmas treats handed down through the generations.

Marriages are often cultural mergers. When I married John, he came as a package deal with a rolling-pin-waving Slovak Grandma Rimarchik. When she died years later at ninety-five, John's mom asked me if there was anything I wanted to remember Grandma by. As the youngest in the line of five daughters-in-law to be asked, I could not believe my luck. I asked for (and got) her ancient sifter and that beautiful solid-oak rolling pin. There's a whole lifetime of flour and sugar, hopes and worries rolled right into the wood. I use it all the time. I keep it oiled and ready for baking emergencies and broken hearts. Best. Inheritance. Ever.

Grandma came to America from Czechoslovakia in 1929. She already had two little girls

coction, had rolling pins all across the tops of hers. I still have one of hers in my file after all these years. Elsie Clark's, the minister's wife, were usually a little stained, wrinkly, and messy . . . bless her heart. But the recipes on them were always delicious and that was all that really counted.

By the time I was fourteen, I had a bunch of recipes in my own little recipe file tucked away for safekeeping for "when I was grown." That file box came with me to my first apartment, and eventually to this old New England farmhouse. The little blue-and-white box is another one of the things I would save in a fire. Though I really hope no one ever tests me on this. I've got a lot of Christmas ornaments to get out already.

Back at the beauty shop, some of those December weeks we were there for three or four hours, because everything got so backed up with all the recipe trading. No one seemed to mind. By noon, all the sets would be finished and it seemed like everyone would get the same idea at the same time. They would all stand up in unison and offer up their cheeks for quick airy kisses so as not to mess up their hair. Then they headed off in all directions. These ladies had weekly errands, which now included the grocery store to buy ingredients for all those new recipes. The week's baking would begin all over again.

The ladies brought their grandmothers' recipes to the shop as well. These were always longer and more complicated than their modern counterparts. They used real butter and whole milk. I learned at the beauty shop that if you are making your grandmother's chocolate cake and something tastes off? Look at your milk. Grandma didn't have 2 percent.

These recipes might have been more involved than the current popular cookie, but they were also always more delicious, with one thing in common. Somewhere along the way there was a Christmas memory. Maybe it was seeing a new sled propped in the corner while you had a bite of that coffee cake in your mouth, or a long Saturday of Christmas baking with Mom, or maybe it was the year Dad came home from the war in time for the holiday and Mom's cake was on the table. The memories all merged and conflated until just the smell of that coffee cake was enough to bring on a rush of happy tears and memories.

"Smell that. This coffee cake smells just like snow."

Now, you or I might think it smelled like brown butter and pecans. But that's because we weren't in on the whole memory trip. And that's what every one of those women in the beauty shop had always been aiming for. They wanted to create memories that would live on in

their kids and their grands long after they were gone. Christmas was their legacy. Women have always been the keepers of Christmas. We are the ones who make it all happen.

John's Slovak grandmother has been with us for twenty-eight years now. She is known all over southern Vermont. Her nut roll sits proudly on the old pharmacist's counter in the middle of our kitchen every Easter and every Christmas Eve without fail. Some years, I have had to get up in the middle of the night after too many winter wines have sent me to bed too early to knead and bake. In the middle of the night, the Grandma Rimarchik alarm goes off. I get up and head down in my nightgown. I find my slippers before turning on the oven and opening the door a crack to keep myself warm. I put on a little Ella Fitzgerald and make the dough that I will punch down and bake come morning so that the warm smells of nutmeg and cinnamon wake up the rest of the house. I am just like the beauty shop ladies. I suspect maybe we all are, at least a little. I want my children to remember those nut rolls and how I learned to bake them from their great-grandma on a hot day in August because I loved their dad. I want them to love someone and be loved that exact same way, and when they see a red plate with nutty buttery goodness . . . I want them to remember.

These Christmas treats are the outline. They

frame the holidays and are freely available to all. Anyone can start the tradition of a cookie party, where each guest brings two dozen cookies so that every person goes home with a plate of someone else's memories hidden inside recipe cards. Or maybe the first Saturday in December can be reserved as sacrosanct for baking with the kids. Grandma comes over with bags of secret ingredients like ginger sugar, and Mom and Dad and the kids all roll up their sleeves and spill flour on the dog and steal bites of dough while making a new tradition.

Butter and Sugar

Here are some favorite Christmas sweets recipes to get you started. I sure hope some of you will send me some of yours.

John's Grandmother's Roszke Cookies

Here is a cookie that will make you swoon. John had these every Christmas and Easter throughout his childhood. Now they are also a Christmas memory for all our kids and our friends. These are not just any Christmas cookie. They are profoundly addictive. Grandma Rimarchik's sweet Slovak brand of love lives on in her recipes. That is surely not a bad legacy to have.

FOR THE DOUGH

- 6 egg yolks
- ½ pound butter
- 2 tablespoons lard or Crisco
- 6 tablespoons powdered sugar
- 1 teaspoon salt
- 4 cups flour
- 1 cup sour cream
- 2½ teaspoons dry yeast
- ¼ cup warm milk

Powdered sugar and cinnamon for rolling

FOR THE FILLING

- 2 beaten egg whites
- 2 pounds finely chopped pecans

Cream eggs, butter, and lard. Add sugar. Gradually add salt and flour. Then add sour cream. Melt yeast in warm milk and add to mixture. Work dough (add a bit more flour if tacky). Refrigerate overnight.

Remove dough from refrigerator and let sit for ½ hour. Work the dough, and cut into 8 or 9 pieces. Work them. Roll into balls. Let rise ½ hour, and roll and cut into squares.

Prepare filling by mixing together egg whites and pecans. Spread filling over squares and then roll into crescents. Let rise ½ hour after filled.

Preheat oven to 350 degrees. Bake for 20 to 25 minutes. Roll in powdered sugar and cinnamon when cool.

Strawberry Whipped Sensation

This thing is just silly good. I actually tried it for the first time at the beauty shop, when I was about seven years old, amidst the mismatched smells of peroxide and perfume. I loved it anyway. When I grew up, I remember reading the recipe card and thinking it sounded a little trashy. Where I grew up, trashy was sort of a cheerful expression of a minor sin. A good bad thing. I mean in the best possible way. Like a squirt from a can of whipped cream or dunking your Oreos in a glass of ice-cold milk. Trashy equals good.

Then I made it. Trashy or not, people love it. You can do a lemon version with a thin layer of lemon pudding filled with tiny bits of sugared lemon. That's pretty tasty, too.

Makes 12 servings or so, depending on who's eating

Butter and then line an 8 x 4-inch loaf pan with aluminum foil or parchment paper.

Remove stems and bruises from strawberries. Roughly mash strawberries in large bowl. Stir in condensed milk, lemon juice, and 2 cups of the Cool Whip. Pour into pan.

Combine chopped cookies and melted butter; press cookies gently into strawberry mixture. Cover and freeze at least 6 hours.

To serve, invert onto plate. Remove foil. Frost with remaining Cool Whip. Garnish with sliced strawberries.

INGREDIENTS

Butter for loaf pan

2 cups fresh strawberries (reserve 1 or 2 large berries for garnish)

1 can (14 ounces) sweetened condensed milk

¼ cup fresh lemon juice

1 tub (8 ounces) Cool Whip, thawed, divided

8 chocolate sandwich cookies (I use Oreos), finely chopped

1 tablespoon butter, melted

Lorraine's Chocolate Icebox Cake

Back to trashy. My mom had an icebox cake for just about every church potluck. She always said the desserts other ladies brought were boring, and they expected her pies so she liked to mix things up. Most icebox cakes had a cookie layer. This one has a sweet nut layer. And yes, it is a little trashy, but boys howdy it sure is good.

FOR THE CRUST

1½ cups flour

1 cup finely chopped walnuts or pecans or a mix of both (use rolling pin or food processor)

1½ sticks butter

FOR THE FILLING

2 small boxes instant chocolate pudding

16 ounces whipped cream cheese

2¾ cup powdered sugar

2 cups heavy cream

1 teaspoon good vanilla

1 tablespoon sugar to taste

Cocoa powder for sprinkling, optional

Preheat oven to 350 degrees.

Combine flour and nuts. Melt butter and add to nut mixture, stirring well. Using your fingers, press nut mixture into a 9 x 11-inch baking dish. Bake for 10 to 15 minutes, until golden brown. Remove from oven and let cool completely.

Prepare instant pudding according to package directions and set aside. In a mixer, combine cream cheese and powdered sugar to desired consistency. Then make whipped cream with heavy cream, vanilla, and sugar.

Once crust has cooled, add cream cheese mixture as first layer, then chocolate pudding, and then finally the whipped cream. Sprinkle cocoa powder on top if desired.

Pig Candy

Bacon and chocolate. What could possibly go wrong? The first time I made this John and I got the giggles while we ate it. It is giggly kind of food. You won't eat very much of it. You can't. But I promise you this. You are gonna laugh.

If you cut the bacon slices in half this will go further at a party, and really, one whole slice is almost too much of a good thing.

INGREDIENTS

3 (4 ounce) bars semisweet chocolate, chopped

1 (4 ounce) bar really dark (70 percent cocoa or more) unsweetened chocolate, chopped

16 slices good bacon (I love applewood-smoked), thick-cut, cooked crisp and cooled.

Melt both the semisweet chocolate and dark chocolate in a double boiler. (You can make a double boiler by boiling a pot of water and putting the chocolate in a pan on top.) Whisk the chocolate until completely smooth. Remove from the heat.

Dunk the bacon into the chocolate, making sure each piece is completely coated. Let excess chocolate drip off, then lay bacon on a cookie tray lined with parchment paper. Put the sheet tray in the refrigerator to set for about 20 to 30 minutes. (If you're just dyin' for a piece you can stick it in the freezer, but watch the time: maybe ten minutes?)

Transfer pieces to a serving platter and try hard not to eat it all before the company comes.

Chestnut Mousse

Just the sound of the word "chestnut" feels like Christmas, doesn't it? You might not always have carolers strolling the streets and a guy roasting nuts on the corner in the village green, but you can always have this.

Bring 1 cup milk, chestnuts, and salt to a simmer. Partially cover, and cook until chestnuts are really soft and milk is reduced, maybe 15 minutes. Transfer chestnut mix to food processor or mixer, and mix until very smooth and velvety. Refrigerate for about an hour.

Mix water with sugar and bring to a boil until syrup is 238 degrees. In a mixer, combine egg yolks and syrup and beat until cool, pale, and fluffy, maybe 7 to 8 minutes. Add cream to a separate bowl and beat into a soft-peaked whipped cream.

Whisk egg and syrup mixture into chestnut puree. Whisk until smooth, then fold in whipped cream.

Put in ramekins, cover tightly with plastic wrap, and chill for at least a couple of hours.

INGREDIENTS

1   cup whole milk plus 1 tablespoon
1   (10 ounce) jar chestnuts
½   teaspoon salt
⅓   cup water
½   cup sugar
2   large egg yolks
⅔   cup heavy cream

Club Night Apricot Horns

I don't think my mom much enjoyed making these. She referred to them as a complicated cookie. There was a waiting period, was probably why. Mom did not like to wait. I get that. I've cheated on the waiting time plenty of years. But it doesn't matter all that much. They are a forgiving cookie. She made them every year when it was her turn to host club at Christmas though. You know if a cookie made the annual December club meeting it must be a good cookie. You invented for Christmas club. You didn't just turn out something from someone else's filebox. You got points for presentation and creativity. And my mama was nothing if not a competitor.

You can change the nuts around here if you want. Almonds are best unless you don't have any, in which case pecans work just fine. So do walnuts. These are never the cookie anyone lists first as their favorite. They don't have the flash of the Linzer or the comfort of the chocolate chip. But I promise you, folks will clean the plate. And the next day two or three of the women from the party will call you up to ask for this recipe.

Unless you're cooking for a lot of people, you might want to halve this one. (Halved, the recipe will still give you about 50 horns!)

Make the dough. Combine butter, cream cheese, and flour in bowl and mix with your hands. Roll dough into 1-inch balls. Refrigerate overnight or until firm (several hours).

In the meantime, make the filling. Combine apricots and sugar in pot and add enough water to cover. Bring to a boil, then reduce to simmer and cook until apricots are tender. Drain and place in refrigerator to cool, then puree. Refrigerate puree until it's time to roll out dough and assemble the horns.

To roll out and assemble the horns, work with 10 balls at a time, keeping the rest in refrigerator so that dough remains firm.

FOR THE DOUGH

1   pound (4 sticks) butter, room temperature

1   pound (2 8-ounce packages) cream cheese, room temperature

4   cups sifted flour

continued on next page

continued from previous page

FOR THE FILLING

1   pound apricots, fresh (halved and pitted) or dried

2   cups sugar

FOR ROLLING

1½   cups chopped nuts (my mom used almonds)

1   cup powdered sugar and more for sprinkling

2   egg whites, slightly beaten

Mix together nuts and powdered sugar. Set up an assembly line of dough balls, apricot puree, beaten egg whites, and powdered sugar and nut mixture. Roll each ball into a 3-inch round. Spread apricot filling on dough. *Less is more here!* The filling will ooze out all over the place and create a huge mess otherwise (but you do want to see it peeking out the sides of the cookie). Roll dough into the shape of a horn (triangle crescent).

Preheat oven to 350 degrees.

One by one, dip horns into the beaten egg whites, then roll in the mixture of chopped nuts and powdered sugar. Place horns on a cookie sheet covered with parchment paper (easier cleanup!). Bake for 12 to 14 minutes or until lightly browned. Remove horns from pan and cool on a rack. Dust liberally with powdered sugar.

Grandma Lorraine's Golden Tassles

As I might have mentioned, when I was growing up, Mom had a pie bakery in our basement, and so inventing a cookie in a pastry dough was just a natural extension of all the buttery goodness going on down there. Kind of a combination of cheesecake and pie, in tiny little easy-to-eat muffin shapes. By the time Christmas arrived we were eating them warmed up for breakfast and cold for lunch. My husband once claimed he gained fifteen pounds from golden tassles alone. They are completely irresistible.

Makes 48 tassles

To make the dough, cream together the butter and cream cheese, then gradually stir in the flour, about ¼ cup at a time. Pinch off pieces of dough and roll into small balls about 1 inch in diameter. Put each ball in the well of a mini muffin pan and press dough against bottom and sides, lining up evenly.

Preheat oven to 350 degrees.

Make the filling. Put cream cheese in mixer and blend well. In ½-cup increments, gradually add the 2 cups of sugar, beating well. Add vanilla and eggs, and beat until very creamy. Spoon into tassies, and bake for 18 to 20 minutes.

Just before serving, top with a dollop of sour cream and a lick of your favorite preserves.

FOR THE DOUGH

2   sticks butter at room temperature
6   ounces cream cheese at room temperature
2   cups flour

FOR THE FILLING

12 ounces cream cheese at room temperature
2   cups sugar
½   teaspoon vanilla
2   eggs at room temperature

FOR THE TOPPING

Sour cream

Fruit preserves

Maple Pecan Cookies

These are my Vermonty thing. When we got up here I felt like I needed to invent some cookie traditions to go with the geography. Maple might have been the obvious choice, but did I mention subtlety has never been my forte? It works.

INGREDIENTS

2   cups flour

1½   teaspoons baking powder

½   teaspoon salt (use a little more if you want; I always do)

¾ cup butter at room temperature

¼   cup light brown sugar

¾   cup dark brown sugar

1   egg

1   teaspoon maple extract

½   cup chopped pecans

Line cookie sheets with parchment paper.

Mix together flour, baking powder, and salt.

In a separate bowl, cream butter and sugars till fluffy (about 3 minutes), then add the egg and maple extract and beat for 3 or 4 more minutes until mixture is very light and fluffy. Add the dry ingredients and just barely mix. Refrigerate for about 30 minutes.

Preheat oven to 350 degrees.

Scoop dough onto cookie sheets by rounded teaspoons and flatten just a little. Bake for about 12 minutes.

Eggnog Gooey Butter Cookies

Hannah loved eggnog when she was little. Starting just after Christmas I would mix it up a couple of mornings every week for breakfast and she would lick the blender. A cookie just seemed like the next natural step, so we made up this recipe together when she was in first grade. It used boxed cake mix—we use golden butter or yellow. We liked them from the very first batch and so we've just kept the recipe the same all these years. One year we figured out that you can frost them too with a little butter, eggnog, and powdered sugar. They are pretty divine either way.

A word about ground nutmeg: Buy the whole ones and grate them. It's cheaper and in all ways tastier besides.

Preheat oven to 350 degrees. In a large bowl with an electric mixer, beat the cream cheese and butter until smooth. Beat in the egg. Mix in the rum extract and nutmeg. Lastly, mix in the cake mix until thoroughly incorporated. Cover bowl and refrigerate for 2 hours.

Roll the chilled batter into 1-inch-sized balls and then roll them in powdered sugar. Place on an ungreased cookie sheet, 2 inches apart. Bake 12 minutes. The cookies will remain soft and gooey. Cool completely and sprinkle with more powdered sugar (more is always better).

INGREDIENTS

- 1 package (8 ounces) cream cheese, room temperature
- ½ cup butter, room temperature
- 1 egg
- 1½ teaspoons rum extract
- ¼ teaspoon ground nutmeg
- 1 package yellow cake mix
- ½ cup powdered sugar and more for sprinkling

Grandma Dorothy's
Best Chocolate Chip Cookies Ever

Dorothy always has a big jar of these on the counter at Christmas. I tried to copy the recipe at home. I added extra chocolate chips. I played around with the eggs. No good. Hers were better. Finally I asked her. "What is the secret to these cookies?" "No regular sugar, hon. Just brown. And twice as many chocolate chips." All I had to do was ask. Maybe in a few generations a bunch of new grandkids will think they are mine. Or maybe yours. Meanwhile, you better double the batch.

Makes 70 cookies

Preheat oven to 375 degrees.

Mix together flour, brown sugar, baking soda, and salt and set aside.

Combine butter, eggs, and vanilla, mixing with a fork so it doesn't get too creamy, then add the dry ingredients, and then the chocolate chips. Refrigerate dough for a little while if it seems too creamy. Drop by the teaspoonful one inch apart and bake about 9 minutes. Remove from pan immediately and cool on wire rack.

INGREDIENTS

2 ¾ cups flour

1½ cups light brown sugar

¾ teaspoon baking soda

2 teaspoons salt (our little secret)

3 sticks butter at room temperature

2 eggs

1½ teaspoons vanilla

4 cups (2 12-ounce packages) semisweet chocolate chips

Santa's Shortbread

We always left carrots out for the reindeer, along with milk and cookies for Santa. We figured that after racing around the world all night, they were all probably ready for a snack. In our favorite *Jolly Old Santa Claus* book there was a picture of what looked like it might be a plate of shortbread. So we decided Santa must love shortbread. That's how these got their name. Believe me, they really are good enough for Santa. I don't like crumbly shortbread, so these have a creamy texture and a subtle flavor.

INGREDIENTS

2   cups flour
1¼ teaspoons salt
2   sticks sweet butter
½   cup powdered sugar
1   teaspoon pure vanilla
      (use Madagascar, it
      really is better)
Seeds scraped out of
      1 vanilla bean, diced
Chopped pecans or walnuts,
      optional, a couple of
      handfuls

Whisk together the flour and salt.

In a separate bowl, beat the butter until it is fluffy (4 minutes). Add the sugar, and beat until mixture is pale and fluffy. Beat in vanilla and teeny-tiny diced vanilla seeds. Beat for a couple minutes more. Add the flour mixture until it is just mixed in and dough sticks together. If your Santa likes nuts, add them now.

Separate the dough into two round balls. Wrap in plastic and refrigerate until firm, about an hour.

Preheat the oven to 325 degrees.

Roll the dough out until it is about ¼-inch thick. Cut into whatever shapes you want. Bake until firm and golden, about 13 minutes.

Spicy Hot Cocoa

Come winter, Grandma McIlvoy would have a pot of cocoa on the stove when I walked home after school. It seemed like maybe she just always had a pot of cocoa going. She was small and round with a halo of white hair. Mrs. Claus could have easily been her sister. So it just figured that she would be an expert cocoa maker. One year when we all had Christmas colds she added a little cinnamon and pepper to the pot to help us breathe better. This is my evolution of that sweet remedy.

Serves 2

In a small bowl mix together vanilla, salt, cinnamon, cocoa, and chocolate chili powder and divide between two mugs. Bring milk to a boil, and pour over cocoa mixture in mugs.

Serve as is, or top with homemade whipped cream with a dash of vanilla, or the best marshmallows you can find. (Even better, make 'em yourself! It's a fun activity with the kids.)

INGREDIENTS

½ teaspoon vanilla

2 teaspoons salt

¼ teaspoon cinnamon

4 heaping tablespoons of good dark cocoa

1 teaspoon chocolate chili powder

2 cups milk

Homemade Marshmallows

You don't have to go to a Parisian confectionary for these. They are simple and delicious and everyone will think you slaved. Let them. And the kids can doctor them up—cocoa is good, so are tiny peppermint crumbs. I have used dabs of cinnamon and the teensiest bit of cayenne to make spicy cocoa with great results.

INGREDIENTS

- 3 packages unflavored gelatin
- 1 cup ice-cold water, divided
- 1½ cups sugar
- 1 cup light corn syrup
- ¼ teaspoon sea salt
- 1 teaspoon vanilla extract
- ¼ cup powdered sugar
- ¼ cup cornstarch
- Butter for baking pan

Put the gelatin into the bowl of a stand mixer along with ½ cup of the water.

In a small saucepan, combine the remaining ½ cup water, sugar, corn syrup, and salt. Place over medium-high heat, cover, and cook for 3 to 4 minutes. Uncover, and keep cooking till mixture reaches 240 degrees. This will take about 7 or 8 minutes. Once at 240 degrees, remove from heat.

Turn the mixer on low and pour the sugar syrup down the side of the bowl into the gelatin mixture. Once you have added all of the syrup, raise speed to high. Mix until thick and lukewarm, which will take about 12 to 15 minutes. Add the vanilla during the last bit of whipping.

While batter is mixing, get your pans ready. Combine the powdered sugar and cornstarch in a small bowl. Butter a 13 by 9-inch baking pan. Add some of the sugar and cornstarch mixture to the pan and roll it around to completely coat the bottom and sides of the pan. Set aside remaining sugar and cornstarch mixture.

After the marshmallow batter is mixed, pour batter into the pan, using a lightly oiled spatula for spreading evenly into the pan. Dust the top with enough of the remaining sugar and cornstarch mix to lightly cover. Reserve the rest. Allow the marshmallows to sit uncovered for at least 4 hours, or overnight.

Turn the marshmallows out onto a cutting board and cut into 1-inch squares using a pizza wheel dusted with the sugar and cornstarch mixture. (Alternatively, the kids can use small cookie-cutters and make fun shapes like stars or little trees.) Once cut, lightly dust all sides of each marshmallow with the rest of the sugar and cornstarch mixture (mix up more if you need it).

Marshmallows will keep in an airtight container for about a month.

Salted Caramel Turtles

Turtles are expensive in the candy shops, but it turns out they are easy and affordable to make. Salted caramel is all the rage for a very good reason. I started adding sea salt to these a couple of years ago. Now my friends all ask me to tell them when I am making them.

Makes 16 turtles

INGREDIENTS

⅔ cup chopped pecans, toasted

4-ounce block of caramel, cut into 16 pieces; or 16 fat caramels (I get mine from Mother Myrick's; see Appendix II, New England Flavors)

16 bittersweet chocolate disks (1- to 1½-inches— I like Guittard's baking wafers)

A pinch of fleur de sel or other coarse sea salt, to garnish each candy

Preheat the oven to 325 degrees.

Divide the pecans into 16 small piles on a parchment-lined or lightly greased baking sheet (a scant 2 teaspoons pecans each).

Flatten each caramel cube into the size of a half dollar and place one on top of each pecan pile. Heat in the oven for 2 to 3 minutes, until the caramel softens and begins to melt. Remove from the oven; wait a minute, then top each cluster with one disk of chocolate, gently pressing it into the softened caramel. Top each candy with a few flakes of fleur de sel. Return tray to oven briefly to melt chocolate.

Allow the caramel and chocolate to cool and set before removing candies from the pan.

Batman and the Indian Chief

When Benjamin was about three years old, my mom made him a Batman costume for Halloween. It was the best present he had ever gotten. He wore it constantly.

Sometimes to preschool. Once to church.

She had to make him a bigger size twice before he tired of it two years later. That boy *was* Batman. Later, at about age six or seven, he graduated to Indian Warrior. We had been to a Renaissance festival and he'd brought home feathers, a loincloth, and some paints. It was not exactly warm as clothing goes. Luckily, it was summer.

Years after his Batman and Indian personas had been left behind, we wandered into a florist one Christmas. Benjamin was about fifteen and a little quiet that year. We were in the height of the uncommunicative, sullen teenage phase, but it was Christmas Adventure. So he dragged his feet but tromped around all the sights with us. He'd lobbied not to go. He'd lost the debate.

One of us had pointed out that "Christmas Adventure is sacred family time, buddy."

"No one else has to do this."

"Well, we are a family and this is just what we do."

It may not have been a very convincing point, but it was the only one I had.

We had already been to Famous-Barr to see the Christmas Bears. We stood in line to see Santa for his little brother, and his younger sister had wanted to stop in at a salon she saw on the street to get some sparkly nail polish for her own Christmas picture with Santa.

It was hard to be a teenage boy around here that year. Nothing we did was very cool.

And so there we were, wandering around a very merry, very Christmasy florist shop. They had an Olde English Santa in long, flowing velvet robes, walking around serving cookies and cocoa. There was jolly Christmas music playing, and I was probably too loudly singing along. I imagine we were getting on that boy's last teenage nerve.

But then we went upstairs to the part of the store where the German glass ornaments hung from tall trees in a little forest-like display. And there they were.

They were both on one tree. Back to back. It was like my very own Christmas miracle. It looked like maybe we had staged it. There was the shiny head of a regal Indian chief, and one branch over, Batman!

Benjamin's face lit up. He was no longer a crabby teenager. He was instantly transformed into the little boy who loved fantasy and us. Our rule was that everyone got one new ornament every year. John saw what was happening and changed the rule immediately to two. Carefully wrapped in layers of white sparkly tissue paper, Benjamin carried them in his own beribboned sack. A bag of memories and promises that said all this teenage stuff was only temporary. 'Cause it was Christmas, and this was sacred family time.

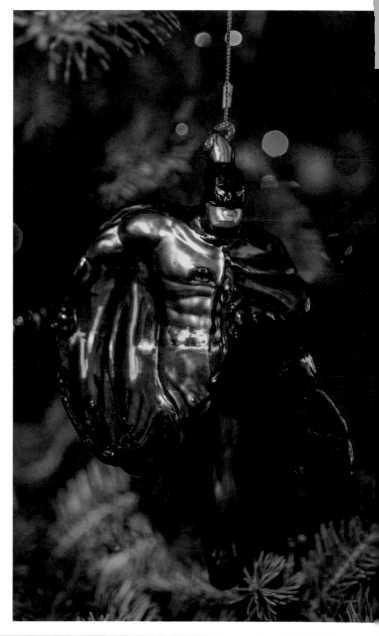

Chapter Three

Jingle Bells

You know those people who go away Christmas week? They come back with stories of beaches and pictures of exotic fruits and vegetables from colorful markets, and photos of drinks with little umbrellas in them. They look robust. They never have any stories about a brother-in-law who had too much to drink on Christmas Eve and argued with your husband about a basketball game or the next election. No one would have brought up the time when the older brother, while babysitting, tried to smother the younger brother with a pillow, thereby ruining their relationship for life. Or that he voted for Ross Perot, so what do you expect?! None of that from those people who go away. They have stories about balmy temperatures and a new recipe for mango shrimp.

But, you know what? I always secretly feel a little sorry for them. Because while it is true that those of us who celebrate the holidays with our families will occasionally have some messy bits to traverse, our team also has the stories of the night we all sat in front of the fire with eggnog and squinted at the tree, looking for light formations. It's like cloud-dreaming only in colorful lights. One year I saw a flying dinosaur in those lights. I can still recall the smell of wood smoke and the sound of the kids playing on the rug with the dogs from that exact moment. Some of our sweetest and best memories come from the dangerous proximity and happenstance of the holidays. We do go away, as I mentioned, that first weekend in December for our own annual Adventure. So I can easily imagine the closeness and memory making of Christmas travel. I have a friend whose family had been ravaged by a messy divorce and another whose husband's death made holiday merrymaking complicated and hard. Both of those families opted for Christmas travel as a way to create new kinds of happy memories. Those families loved Christmas and wanted to love it still, only in a new-fashioned way. So they chose a traditional destination and counted on the newness of the geography to distract them from what was missing. In both cases the reports were happy ones. They still missed what had come before, but they were able to savor the missing in the midst of the new.

If your family is looking for a good travel destination that really feels like Christmas, then New England is just made for you. We've got the snow and the piney forests right up next to the quaint villages and charming local festivals. We have hunters bringing the turkey to the table and syrup makers trying out their new glaze recipes at the Christmas fair. In Concord, Massachusetts, there's even a cheese parade that features the largest hunk of Parmigiano-Reggiano in the United States riding in honor right in front of Santa's sleigh. You're not going to see that anywhere else.

Around here, the kids can go sledding and the adults can find a hot buttered rum beside a cozy fire. Everyone can enjoy a night under the stars on a horse-drawn sleigh with a Vermonter who knows his stars. In a landscape filled with snow, Mom and Dad can get up early and have a romantic morning sleigh ride of their own.

We usually have a couple of feet of snow, with drifts of four to five. The nighttime mountains are big fat cartoon outlines against all that snow. We get little flurries most mornings and the whole place sparkles like an enchanted forest.

The snow pants, hats, and mittens are always piled on the radiators, and our mudroom is filled with boots. We have extra pairs of everything, so when visitors come unprepared they can join in an evening of impromptu sledding. Moonlight sledding keeps us all from getting bored when the sun goes down at four in the afternoon. We go to sleep tired and happy.

There are no streetlights here in Vermont. Newcomers tend to fret about that. We did. But pretty soon everyone adores the pleasure of the night sky and the wildlife freely roaming under the cover of night. On the best nights, we get to watch the deer jumping through open fields of snow. Watching their silhouettes run so fast and step so high on that expanse of white brings to mind those polar reindeer. They fairly fly.

The animals are less hidden, more vulnerable, in the sparkly winter world where the branches are only sharp outlines in an all-white landscape. Their obvious presence reminds us to fill the feeders, and makes us feel lucky and blessed to share their space.

When the moon is full and the ground is covered with snow, there is enough natural light outside to see the color and pattern of a

small child's mittens at fifty feet. During hard snows, we often have fog drifting in along with the flakes. On those nights, the darkness seems to amplify the distance between us and the rest of the world. It is peaceful and beautiful. There are fewer places that make us want to leave here anymore, not even for a while.

But here's something they don't tell you before you move to your isolated mountain paradise. Winter is loud. At first there are those silent snowfalls and you are deeply in love. You stand amidst the tall pines watching millions of those fat flakes fall and swirl to the ground. There is so much beauty amidst so much action that the silence in comparison is amazing.

Then, too, there are those bright blue days when the temperature is five below, and through all that cold sunshine you can see for miles and the air is so still and so quiet that you find yourself using words like "awesome." Words that the kids use to describe good pizza, but that you used to reserve for Christmas Eve and singing "Silent Night" with a baby in your arms.

At first winter is a quiet lover and you cannot get enough. Only after you have been here a while, and are no longer just a weekender, do you get the real story. Because in between those cold weeks are days when the temperatures climb into the thirties and the ice on your slate roof begins its secret melt. Then one evening, just as you are settling into the tub, it happens.

WHOMP. The sound of the ice sliding off your roof makes a hurricane seem quiet. Windows rattle. Slate tiles fly off, too, of course, which is why the roofers up here all have such big cushy houses. Your animals hide under the beds. You run outside, and a sheet of ice narrowly misses taking off your arm. You run right back in.

Sometimes a shutter gets hit, and hangs lopsidedly the rest of the winter waiting for repair. You can't fix it, because the day after the warmup there's a cold snap and an ice storm, making climbing perilous again. And meanwhile, the ice is burrowing under your slate roof and there are drips in your old 1838

farmhouse ceilings that no pots and pans can solve.

John Haynes, our tree guy, is the only one brave enough to get up there. He rakes and shovels and stops the slate tiles from lifting. He keeps the drips from turning our winter farmhouse into a rainforest. Everyone needs a John Haynes up here.

The windstorms, too, are louder than anything you ever imagined, growing up in tornado country. We are in a high valley surrounded on all sides by these nurturing Vermont mountains. But the nor'easters that you hear about on the news were invented here, and when you are in the middle of these mountains you are in a wind tunnel.

The wind whips around the house. It yawns and moans. If the temperatures are even a little mixed, you get wind and ice melting at the same time. It feels just like your house is falling down.

Up here, you have to consciously celebrate winter every chance you get, or the cabin fever and steady beat of frigid gray landscape can chill your soul. John and I went out for an early-morning sleigh ride on a day of brittle cold sunshine this year. We snuggled underneath thick blankets, with only the sounds of the swish and jangle of the tack intruding on the quiet landscape. There was the quiet whoosh of the leather bindings, and the bridles jangling, a soft bassline and percussion to our morning. The crystal coating the trees was almost like a cartoon shouting CHRISTMAS IN NEW ENGLAND! We had scheduled the ride not knowing Vermont would be recording record-low temperatures, but it actually turned out not to matter. We could smell the horsey steam coming off our team and we got to see the fox and bunny tracks beside the streams as the woodland critters made their morning pilgrimages out for breakfast. It felt like the best and oldest kind of Christmas Adventure. We held hands and quietly soaked up all that sparkly wintry landscape and made ready for all that was surely coming.

If Christmas or winter travel is in your future, New England will reliably deliver charm and tradition and memories that will count. In the back of this book, you'll find a few of our family's favorite winter and holiday activities with a focus on our home state, Vermont (see Appendix I, Winter Adventures in Vermont).

Cabin Food

If you rent a cabin in the North Country mountains for the weekend, at some point you are probably going to want to cook. So here are a few easy recipes that will practically cook themselves. Perfect for your weekend in Vermont.

John's Famous Chili

I know yours is good. But just wait till you taste this one. This is the kind of supper that you will find yourself thinking about later. It has a robust meaty flavor with just the right amount of heat. And can I just say how perfectly gorgeous it looks in an old cast-iron pot? That's worth something too. I call for cubes of beef and pork but you could also use ground beef and ground pork.

Cut beef and pork into 1-inch cubes.

In a large bowl, combine flour with salt and pepper. Add meat and toss to coat. In a large skillet over medium-high heat, cook the meat in the oil, stirring often. Add the onions and garlic and sauté until vegetables are softened. Add the water and tomato paste and simmer for 1 hour (less if using ground meat).

Soak the dried chiles in hot water for 15 to 20 minutes. Process soaked chile peppers in a blender with just enough of the soaking water to make a pureé. Strain out excess liquid. Add pureé to meat mixture along with jalapeño, kidney beans, brown sugar, and cumin. Simmer 1½ to 2 hours longer. Salt to taste.

Serve with "The Boys": My great pal Julia Reed told me that in the South, curry toppings are always called "The Boys." I loved this so much I started using it the next day as if I had been saying it my whole life. I think it is just about a perfect fit for chili toppings, too.

The Boys

Oyster crackers
Shredded cheese
Green onions
Sour cream

2   pounds stew beef

1   pound pork shoulder

½   cup flour

½   teaspoon salt

¼   teaspoon pepper

3   tablespoons vegetable oil

2   medium onions, chopped

6   cloves garlic, minced

4   cups water

1   small can tomato paste

2   medium dried ancho chiles, stems and seeds removed

5   dried red New Mexican chiles, stems and seeds removed

1   hot jalapeño or serrano chile, seeds removed, finely chopped, more or less to your taste

3   cans dark red kidney beans

Brown sugar to taste, 1 cup at least

1½ teaspoons ground cumin (or chili powder)

Salt to taste

Potato Leek Soup

Soup is perfect for winter. You know how sometimes the produce section at the grocery store looks so downtrodden in the winter? You are craving some tomatoes or beets. You can barely remember how corn tastes. Maybe just one good peach. Well, look to the larder vegetables. These are always fresh and good and you can make a hearty, soul-satisfying soup with the greens that still taste as fresh as summer. No two batches of this ever taste the same. Sometimes I throw in a whole cup of chives or tarragon. Maybe lardoons or pancetta. I almost always drizzle little splatters of fresh cream on top with a few fresh chives.

INGREDIENTS

- 1 pound leeks (4 to 5 medium), cleaned and dark green sections removed
- 3 tablespoons sweet butter

Kosher salt

- 14 ounces (3 small) Yukon Gold potatoes, peeled and diced
- 1 quart vegetable broth
- 1 cup heavy cream
- 1 cup buttermilk
- ½ teaspoon white pepper
- 1 tablespoon fresh snipped chives

Chop the leeks into small pieces. Rinse carefully. Leeks are notorious for the amount of dirt they hang onto and you don't want a mouthful of mud in this recipe.

In a pot over medium heat, melt butter. Add leeks and a heavy pinch of salt and let the leeks sweat for 5 minutes. Decrease the heat to medium-low and cook until the leeks are tender, about 25 minutes, stirring occasionally.

Add the potatoes and the vegetable broth and increase heat, bringing broth to a boil. Reduce the heat to low, cover, and gently simmer until the potatoes are soft, approximately 45 minutes.

Turn off the heat and puree the mixture with an immersion blender until smooth. Stir in the heavy cream, buttermilk, and white pepper. Taste and adjust seasoning if desired. Sprinkle with chives and serve immediately.

Cardamom Tapioca Pudding

This is the most comforting sweet food I know. It will settle both a crabby child and the parents of one.

INGREDIENTS

1 cup tapioca

4 cups cold water

5 cups milk

1 cup heavy cream

2 egg yolks

⅔ cup sugar

Zest of 1 lemon

2 pinches salt

1 teaspoon cardamom, or more to taste

Combine tapioca and water in a bowl and refrigerate overnight. In the morning, combine milk and tapioca in saucepan and add cream, egg yolks, sugar, zest, salt, and cardamom to taste, and put over low heat. Cook as low as possible for a couple of hours. Serve either warm or cold.

Cheddar Ale Soup

This feels like a party in a bowl. You eat this when you want to watch *Jurassic Park*. Sometimes Christmas movies are just big blockbusters that bring everyone into the room over loud, silly fun. This soup is perfect on that night. Cover it with popcorn and everyone will immediately catch the mood.

Cook bacon, crumble, and set aside.

Over medium heat, melt butter. Add carrot, celery, onion, and bay leaf. When vegetables are translucent, stir in the flour and cook, stirring, for 3 minutes to thicken. Gradually whisk in beer. Stir until mixture is bubbly and thick. Then add milk, stock, Worcestershire, and dry mustard. Bring soup to a simmer, stirring almost constantly so it does not scorch. Add cheese one handful at a time until cheese is melted. Do not let boil.

Remove from heat. Remove bay leaf. Season soup with salt and pepper. For meat lovers, add bacon. For non-meat lovers, top with cooked popcorn. Croutons are good too, but the popcorn is fun and delicious.

INGREDIENTS

- 4 slices bacon
- 4 tablespoons butter
- ¼ cup minced carrot
- ¼ cup minced celery
- ½ cup minced onion
- 1 bay leaf
- ⅓ cup flour
- 1 bottle (12 ounces) medium amber beer
- 2½ cups 2 percent milk
- 1½ cups chicken or vegetable stock
- 1 tablespoon Worcestershire
- 1 teaspoon dry mustard
- 4 cups of seriously sharp cheddar

Salt and pepper to taste

- 1 cup popcorn, optional

Decadent Mac 'n' Cheese

Our kitchen is the most consoling room in our house. We have an old walnut table surround by cushy banquettes where we can all fit no matter how many of us show up. This is never the place I go to add to my to-do list. If anything, I come in here and cross things off. And this is what we eat on the days when I get overwhelmed by a holiday that's rolling by too fast to keep up. It is encouraging food—do-it-yourself therapy. There is never anything much wrong around here that a bowl of this won't help make right. It is also a pretty great party surprise. No one expects mac 'n' cheese, but it is so lip-smacking good, everyone will talk about what a great idea it was. You can add lobster to it if you want to get fancy. But you don't have to. It is a perfect food just as it is. As it bakes, the nutmeg and cheese perfume the steam and people wander into the kitchen from all corners of the house just following their noses.

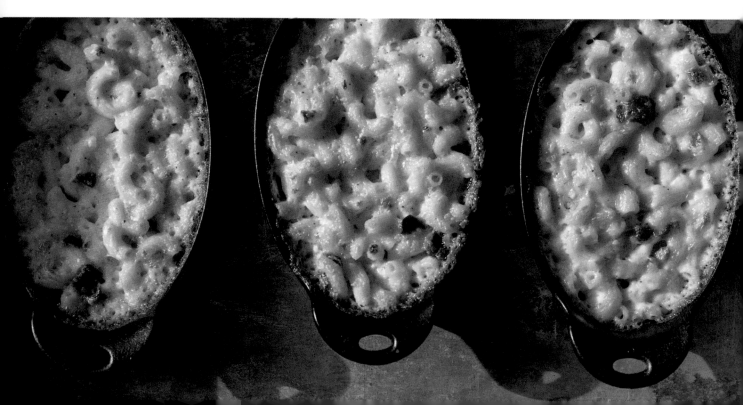

Preheat the oven to 400 degrees.

Cook the macaroni al dente in salty water. Drain, toss with the olive oil, and set aside in a large mixing bowl.

Cut the bacon into ½-inch pieces and sauté over medium heat until brown, but not crisp, about 10 minutes. Drain, then add to the cooked macaroni.

In a medium saucepan, bring the milk just to a foamy boil, then reduce the heat to very low.

In another saucepan, melt the butter over medium heat. When the foam subsides, remove from the heat. Whisk in the flour and continue stirring until a smooth, pale roux has formed. Return the saucepan to medium heat and, while whisking steadily, begin ladling the hot milk into the roux, 1 cup at a time, completely incorporating each cup before adding the next. After all the milk has been added, continue to whisk until the sauce thickens and bubbles gently, about 2 minutes. Add the Parmesan and most of the Gruyère, along with the salt and pepper and nutmeg. Stir until the cheese has completely melted.

Pour the sauce over the macaroni, mix thoroughly, and pour into a buttered 10 by 14-inch gratin dish. (Ramekins work well as individual dishes or maybe use small cast-iron pans . . . ?) Pop in the oven and bake for 12 minutes. Remove, sprinkle remaining Gruyère over the top, and put back in the oven till golden and bubbly, about 10 minutes more.

INGREDIENTS

About a pound of macaroni

A couple of tablespoons olive oil

4 ounces thick cured bacon, preferably from local happy pigs

5 cups whole milk, preferably raw

¼ cup sweet butter

About ½ cup flour

About 1 cup grated hard cheese (I like a local Parmesan when I can get it. Aged 2 years if available.)

2 cups grated Gruyère (sheep or goat is especially lovely here in the mountains. Older cheeses have that wonderful nutty flavor), with a bit reserved for sprinkling

1½ teaspoons good salt (less or more to taste)

½ teaspoon fresh ground pepper

½ teaspoon nutmeg

Root Beer Pulled Pork

This is one time when substitutions should be skipped. Coke does not work. I don't know why. Only that it doesn't. I start eating this as soon as it has cooled enough to pull apart. I make coleslaw the old-fashioned way. In theory, I know that coleslaw is not a winter dish, so I didn't include the recipe here. But if you put it in a sandwich on top of this particular pulled pork, I don't think it counts as a summery food.

I like my coleslaw simple. Just in case you do want to know what that means: I mix a cup of oil and about the same amount of white wine vinegar with 1½ cups of sugar and mix that with a handful of large grated carrots, a couple of diced green peppers, an onion, also diced, and a bunch of chopped celery. I pour it all over a head of grated cabbage. Sometimes I add a little mayo if I want a creamier version, and gobs and gobs of pepper. (Okay, I guess I included the recipe after all.)

INGREDIENTS

3 pounds pork loin roast

Olive oil

Steak seasoning

3 bottles of your favorite strong root beer (not diet)

1 cup brown sugar

3 cloves garlic, minced

Coat meat with olive oil and liberally coat with steak seasoning. Turn the heat on high on the grill or use a cast-iron pan. Sear meat on all sides. Once pork is dark and crusty on each side (don't forget to do the ends!), place in a baking dish.

Preheat oven to 300 degrees.

Cover pork with root beer and coat the top with brown sugar. Sprinkle garlic on top. Cover with foil and bake for about three hours until the meat is falling apart.

Shred pork using two forks and serve on kaiser rolls with a good vinegary coleslaw.

Vermonters' Sugar on Snow

We used to think you ate the snow. We swirled our syrup around in snow and added cream and salt and made some little snow ice-cream concoction. It was good—but what it was not was Sugar on Snow. When we moved to Vermont, we finally got it. The maple hardens into a candy on the snow and the pickles add a fast, sour bite that keeps your palate clear enough for all that sweet syrupy crunchy goodness.

You can't eat very much of this. But you will have fun making it and the children will think you are a snow fairy. Oh, wait. Maybe I just *said* you had to be a snow fairy to make it, and the little ones around here believed me. Okay, okay, there may have been a crown . . .

Pack dishes firmly with snow and place in the freezer until ready to use.

Bring syrup to a boil, about 232 degrees, in a heavy pot. (You can spread butter on the rim of the pot to prevent syrup from boiling over.) Test doneness by dropping a bit of syrup onto the snow; it is ready when it stays on top of the snow and dries. Serve with local bread-and-butter pickles.

You eat the crunchy-syrup bits, not the snow, and those pickles cut the sweetness in between bites!

INGREDIENTS

Fresh powdery snow

2 cups dark (B grade) maple syrup

Mud Season

Well balanced and deceptively potent. Delicious, too. There is a great little book that inspired this drink. Go ahead. Look it up. It is a wonderful stocking stuffer and I promise it will make you laugh. *Mud Season*, by Ellen Stimson. It has its own bunch of delicious recipes, too. Buy one for you and one for your mom and sister. Might as well get a little Christmas shopping done.

INGREDIENTS

- 2 parts Whistlepig Rye, or use your favorite rye
- 1½ parts simple syrup (equal amounts water and sugar simmered on stove until sugar dissolves)
- 1 part good apple cider vinegar
- 2 dashes of your favorite bitters

Mix all ingredients, shaken, not stirred, and served frothy over ice.

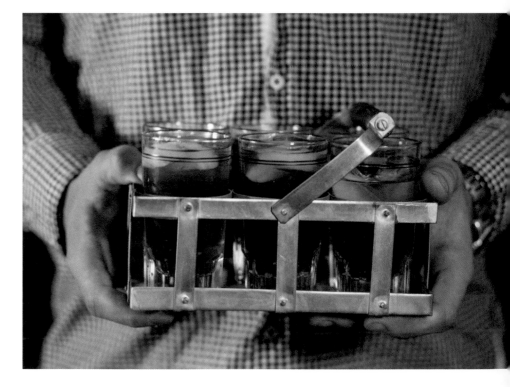

Grandma Rimarchik's Slovak Green Bean and Potato Soup

This is a funny soup. The Hungarian paprika adds a kick, and while it does not make a particularly pretty bowl, it is oddly satisfying. My vegetarian daughter loves it and so do my big strapping sons.

Place the green beans into a pot with enough water to cover. Add the baking soda to the water; bring the liquid to a boil, reduce heat to medium, and cook until the green beans are nearly tender, 7 to 10 minutes. Drain the water from the green beans; set aside.

Place the potatoes in a large pot with enough salted water to cover; bring to a boil, reduce heat to medium, and continue cooking until almost tender, about 20 minutes. Remove from heat, but do not drain the water from the pot.

Heat the butter over medium heat. Cook the onion and bacon bits in the melted butter until the onions are soft and translucent, 5 to 7 minutes; add to the large pot with the potatoes, along with the sour cream, buttermilk, and milk; stir until smooth. Add the green beans. Season with lots of paprika, chives, and salt and pepper.

Place the large pot over low heat and cook the soup at a simmer until hot and the flavors have melded, about 30 minutes.

INGREDIENTS

3   cups fresh green beans, trimmed and cut into 1-inch pieces

1   tablespoon baking soda

1½ cups peeled and diced potatoes

⅓   cup butter

½   cup diced onion

⅓   cup bacon bits

1   pint of sour cream

1   cup buttermilk

2   cups whole milk

Paprika (a bunch)

Chives, fresh if you can find them

Salt and ground black pepper, to taste

Homestyle

Our anniversary falls on December 14, which makes a Christmas ornament the perfect present. John gave me this ornament in celebration of our twentieth year together. It pretty much sums up my whole life. Home and hearth and books. He gets me.

Recently, an author I like, Mark Childress, posted a question on his Facebook page that garnered tons of replies: "If you just found out that the next twenty-four hours are your last on earth . . . what would you do with your day?"

Turns out, I would mostly do the things I already do anyway. I'd whip up a batch of deviled eggs, go for a walk with John and the dogs, make love, and then have supper with the kids and tell some funny stories.

This ornament sort of says that.

What? Don't your ornaments talk to you? This one may also be saying, "Hey, kids (not you, Eli, you're too young), your mother would really like to have some fat grandbabies."

But that's a whole nother conversation.

Chapter Four

Christmas Adventure

Did I mention that I started really falling in love with John around Christmastime? It's only fitting, then, that he met my son, Benjamin, for the first time when the three of us went looking for a tree together. I hadn't introduced them sooner because I didn't want to be one of those people whose child meets everyone they date. But things were getting serious. It was time. I called it our Christmas Adventure.

I thought if Benjamin met John outside, he could run wild and they would both have plenty of room to sort out this beginning. John was twenty-four and Benjamin was two and a half. There was bound to be some noise. Luckily, John had needed a tree and I knew about a great cut-your-own Christmas-tree forest.

It turned out to be the best meeting I have ever attended. There was canned whipped cream, hot chocolate, hide-and-seek, a pine-cone-throwing contest, a giant tree, and clouds of giggles all day long. I could not believe my happy luck. The two people I loved best loved me back and were well on the way to loving one another. It was a little Christmas magic for sure. Benjamin spent the following afternoon with his dad, while John and I continued our Christmas Adventure, wandering around town looking for ornaments for that giant tree.

Fast-forward to the following year: over the summer, we'd won a night's stay at a fancy downtown hotel. We hung onto that reward till December rolled around and I announced it was time for another Christmas Adventure. It was what we'd called it the year before and I thought it would set a cheery holiday tone. Nothing more. I just started planning another Christmas Adventure.

That weekend, we drove over the bridge to St. Louis and headed straight for Famous-Barr. I wanted Benjamin to see Santa and get his picture taken and we would all wander through Santaland and see the Famous-Barr Bears. They were an annual animated attraction with little bear elves making toys and dipping candies amidst a cheerful Christmasy forest. It was like a miniature holiday Disney scene, and I loved it as much as any kid.

We stayed the night at the hotel, bounced on the beds, got ice from the ice machine fifty times, ate a big jolly holiday brunch, and each of us found one perfect new ornament from a local florist shop, Cumberworth's. They boasted a giant merry-go-round and tons of great decorations. When we came back home to put up the tree the next day, we baked cookies and played Christmas carols and talked nonstop about how this year's Adventure had been so much fun, we should do it every year.

There it was. A tradition was born.

Traditions often start by happenstance. You throw a great holiday party and by the third year you realize all your friends have come to count on it and on you. Or maybe Grandma flies in to bake cookies one year and by the time the kids are teenagers they are inviting their friends to come for Grandma's Cookie Week. We just celebrated our twenty-eighth Christmas Adventure. These weekends are the highlight of my year.

Like vacation, they really are sacred family time. Those we've invited to join in are few and far between. We have had a girlfriend or two here and there, and one erstwhile fiancé made the cut. Briefly. Aunt Patsy, our hip city aunt, got invited one year to a dinner in New York City, and she was such a loving presence that she has been our only repeat guest. She is always with us when we do Adventure in Manhattan. Dates have changed to accommodate the kids, first for college and then emerging professional calendars. Activities vary year to year, too. I have always traveled for my work, and the hotel points I accumulate add up to Christmas Adventure. But there have been leaner years, too, where Adventure was homemade. Those have been as sweet as any of the rest.

One year we made Christmas-tree puppets and filled pinecones with peanut butter for the birds. We dragged our dining room table into the library, built a fire, and had what Hannie afterwards called our "Homespun Adventure." There was fried chicken, mashed potatoes, corn pudding, applesauce, and buttermilk biscuits. I did miss having someone else making those beds, though. And Eli mourned the ice machine.

Now we talk about Christmas Adventure

throughout the year. We dream about where we'll go next. I, for one, am eager to do an Adventure in Maine, where I hear Santa comes in by lobster boat. A Christmas lobster fest deeply appeals.

This is a tradition with long-lasting memories. Even if they are not always stories of a happy family meandering through Christmas-tree forests, sipping hot chocolate, and admiring festive boughs laden with holiday ornaments. Nope. Not always.

For just one example, do you remember the year the movie *Elf* came out?

We were in New York City, in one of those high-rise cinema multiplexes. We were on the highest floor, with about five or six escalators to descend to get back down to street level. We had decided to fit the movie in before dinner, so our dinner reservation got pushed back. Now we were rushing to get to the restaurant.

The kids had all loved the movie, but for some reason Eli, our youngest, probably hungriest, and certainly tiredest member, was grumpy. No one remembers exactly what happened anymore. There was an attempt maybe to ride the escalator handrail. There was a wrestling match that went awry. Really, it was a jumble of bodies. Eli was growling and crying and throwing his body this way and that. Family lore holds that he was trying to bite his sister while she held him at arm's length. We all fell apart laughing. This did not make it better. One of us had the presence of mind to scoop Eli up and hug him while he went on kicking, screeching, and generally acting like a crazed member of Alice Cooper. Then, as quickly as it began, it stopped. He started laughing with the rest of us. We made it to ground level, got into a cab, raced to the restaurant, and got a milkshake in his hands ASAP. And just like that it was over. This calm, sweet little boy who was normally so genial had thrown a spectacular public fit that we are still talking about many years after the fact. We laugh when we tell it. It is a memory no one would have planned, but all of us, even the fit thrower, remembers as a funny moment and a family rally.

We have our fair share of those. I guess everyone probably does. Like, the year of the Christmas Adventure that almost wasn't.

Hannah was engaged to a man she would eventually decide she could not marry. But it was December and the holidays were barreling down on us as they do, whether everyone is feeling very damn merry or not.

It was the twenty-fifth anniversary of this tradition that, as I may have mentioned once or twice, I love practically more than any other family thing we do. I love all the holidays, but Christmas Adventure is so uniquely ours. It is all about lifelong promises kept and expectations of good stuff to come. And this year, Hannah wasn't coming. Not because of scheduling trouble or an illness, but because of strife and conflict in the family. Her fiancé didn't think we wanted him around. (This may have been exacerbated by a comment he unfortunately overheard John make at Thanksgiving, which mainly concerned their dog, for God's sakes.)

Now, this might have been a little irritating. It is possible that I might have minded. The whole mess was sort of snowballing. Dan was feeling unwelcome, and Hannah had been persuaded . . . Oh, who knows? Maybe it was even her idea. But when you feel bad about something your adult kids are doing and you want to blame somebody for it—probably not yourself and probably not your kid—the guy the kid is engaged to becomes the target. Anyway, Hannah had been persuaded that she should stand with Dan in some sort of solidarity.

If he felt unwelcome, then she would stand with him. I can almost admire it. Well, in other people's families. Luckily, after a little traditional holiday arguing, a few tears, and reluctant laughter, we turned it around. And just like that, they were back to coming to Christmas Adventure.

Their dog, Elsie the Great Dane, came along. We stayed in a lovely pet-friendly inn for her and she was a joy to be around.

We went on a snowy sleigh ride and ate an amazing southern dinner at Chef Rogan Lechthaler's place. We had one of our best Christmas Adventure weekends ever. From time to time these things happen. They surely do. Invariably at the holidays. Sometimes you get the holiday memories you want, not always though, and then, sometimes you get even better ones.

Now John and I are what must be described as middle-aged. Half of one hundred can hardly be colored any other way. Still, I have peanut-butter-and-jelly-striped hair, and he has long, superbly cool sideburns. We still seem hip . . . at least to us. I love retelling each other our stories almost as much as I loved living them in the first place. They may even be better in the retelling.

One year we met up in New York City, saw

a live show of *A Prairie Home Companion,* had dinner at Balthazar with Aunt Patsy, and got our ornaments at a place in Union Square. Aunt Patsy is my dear friend (and really part of the family), Patricia Bostleman. Patricia could not be less of a "Patsy" no matter how hard she tried. But because she's part of this family, an ironic nickname was inevitable.

There were the years when we had brunch at a fancy hotel in St. Louis. Those meals required a full-on nap before we could put up the Christmas tree. What's the harm in a little more hollandaise sauce? It's Christmas Adventure, after all. Then maybe just a little nap.

And then there was the year when we froze almost half to death in Chicago. Windy and Freezing City, apparently.

We are reminded of the richness of our traditions and these stories that make up our shared family history each year. Most especially, we are glad for the luck of having fun together. We are even glad of knowing how to fight, fuss, and come back together no matter what. Eventually, the kids will add husbands and wives and grandbabies to our mix. (They better, anyway.) Santa will likely make a comeback.

We called it Christmas Adventure in the beginning because of how that would sound to the ears of a small child. And ever since, we have tried to live up to the name. It has been an adventure . . . all of it. We are all glad to have each other, our colorful past, and this mostly sweet life we still share together.

Homespun Tastes

There are times when a holiday needs a quiet celebration. Maybe there is a new baby and nobody is getting much sleep. Perhaps someone has been sick or there has been a job loss. Or maybe you have just had a run of happy loud celebrating and everyone needs to stay home and snuggle in. These recipes will make all of you feel tended and snug.

Loaded Mashed Potatoes

"Light" is not a word anyone would use here. These potatoes might make you a little sleepy. But if your daughter and her boyfriend have just broken up right before Christmas, this is what you make. If the sister-in-law who hates your dog is coming, these are your answer. And if the other sister-in-law who has the practically all-white house with concrete countertops punctuated by bits of dark distressed leather is staying for the whole holiday weekend . . . make a double batch.

INGREDIENTS

4 Yukon Gold potatoes (about 1½ pounds), quartered

6 tablespoons of butter (This is never enough; I just add until it is a rich golden color.)

Sour cream or cream cheese, optional

Salt and pepper

Chives

Boil potatoes until fork-tender. (I leave the skins on because it gives color, vitamins, and tastes good.) Melt the butter. (For creamier potatoes, add more butter or a bit of sour cheese or cream cheese.)

Combine potatoes and butter in a large bowl and mash with a wooden spoon. Add salt, pepper, and chives to taste.

The biggest mistakes people make here are not using enough salt and mixing too fast in a stand mixer, making the potatoes gummy and gluey. An old-fashioned potato masher works, but a wooden spoon works just fine too.

Corn Pudding

I am crazy for corn pudding. My version is just like your grandmother's. It is not diet food but it will take you right back to her chenille bedspreads and the sound of Bing Crosby on the stereo, complete with the scratches where the needle always got stuck.

INGREDIENTS

- 1 pepper (poblano, jalapeño—your preference)
- 1 red or green bell pepper
- 4 cups cooked corn kernels
- ½ cup whole milk
- 6 eggs, separated
- ½ cup heavy cream
- 6 tablespoons butter, diced; more for the baking dish
- ½ cup sugar
- ¾ cup flour
- 1 teaspoon baking powder
- 2 teaspoons sea salt
- 1 cup shredded sharp cheddar

Preheat oven to 350 degrees. Butter baking dish (maybe 13 x 9) or ramekins. Core, seed, and dice peppers. Roast in oven until blistery. Set aside.

Use food processer to puree corn with milk. Add egg yolks a little at a time, so they get totally mixed in. Then add heavy cream and butter. Add sugar slowly, so mixture gets light and fluffy, maybe 2 minutes. Transfer to a big bowl.

In another bowl, mix flour, baking powder, and sea salt. Fold dry ingredients into corn mixture.

In yet another bowl, beat egg whites until you get soft peaks. Slowly fold egg whites into corn mixture. Fold cheese into corn mixture.

Put corn mixture in baking dish. Spread peppers on top. Bake 40 to 45 minutes until golden brown.

Olive Oil Ice Cream

Once you get the basic ratio of eggs and cream down, you can make any flavor you want. This is a reliable, easy, basic flavor that goes with everything and gives you instant street cred as a fancy cook. It has a silky mouthfeel and a subtle taste that is neither cloying nor uppity. It is just really, really good.

You'll need an ice-cream maker for this one.

Simmer milk and cream and take it off the heat. Do not boil. Set aside.

Whisk egg yolks until they get light. As they lighten, whisk in sugar. Add oil and whisk.

Temper cream mixture into eggs so eggs do not curdle. Whisk together and put back on stove on medium-low heat. Cook and stir until mixture starts to thicken, 5 to 7 minutes.

Refrigerate uncovered until cool. Once cool, refrigerate overnight. (If you're in a rush, 4 hours will do.)

Put mixture in the ice-cream maker and *wham bam!* freeze it.

INGREDIENTS

- 3 cups whole milk
- 1 cup heavy cream
- 6 large egg yolks
- 9 ounces sugar (a little bit more than a cup)
- ½ cup strong-flavored olive oil

Cheddar Chive Biscuits

Here's the trick. You place a trio of little dough balls, about the size of one of those hard, rubbery little super balls, into the wells of a greased muffin tin. You will get perfect beautiful rolls every single time. They taste divine and they look like they belong in a very fancy restaurant.

INGREDIENTS

2 packages rapid-rise yeast

2 teaspoons sugar, divided

1 cup warm water, divided

5 cups flour

2 tablespoons butter, plus more for greasing and melted butter for brushing

2 teaspoons salt

½ cup evaporated milk

2 cups really sharp cheddar cheese, grated

¼ cup chives

Mix yeast with 1 teaspoon sugar and ½ cup of the warm water. Sprinkle a dusting of flour on top. Let stand for 5 to 10 minutes until bubbly.

Combine butter, remaining sugar, salt, remaining water, and milk in mixer. Stir in 1 cup of the flour, add cheese and chives, then add the yeast mixture. Slowly stir in the rest of the flour until the dough comes together.

Turn dough out on a lightly floured surface. Knead for 8 to 10 minutes until dough is smooth and elastic-feeling. Shape it into a ball. Place in greased (buttered) bowl. Flip it over so both sides are greased. Cover with dishtowel and set aside in warm place for 1 hour until it has doubled in size. (If you're pressed for time you can skip this step and go straight to the baking. The biscuits will maybe not rise as high, but they will be fine.)

Remove dough from bowl, turn it out onto floured surface, and punch it out. Then let it rest for 10 minutes.

Butter 3 large muffin tins. Create three balls of the dough for each muffin well. When placed in wells, balls should be touching but not pinched together. Let rise for 30 minutes (but if you're in a hurry, you can skip this step too).

Preheat oven to 375 degrees.

Bake about 20 minutes until the crust is golden brown. When you
remove them from the oven, immediately take them out of the tins (so
the bottoms do not continue to bake) and brush with melted butter.

Crostata

A good crostata is like pie without the fuss. The crust can't break because it isn't really a crust. It is just pillows of sweet dough interspersed with gooey, fruity fillings. Crostata is like the dumpling of the pasta world. Easy and forgiving. Delicious and good. I make these all year long. In the summer I make a blueberry peach, and in the spring, a strawberry rhubarb. And at Christmas I make one with apples and raisins that feels festive and looks like it took real work. It doesn't. But your guests will think it did, which is even better.

FOR THE PASTRY

2 cups flour

⅓ cup sugar

¾ teaspoon good sea salt

½ pound cold sweet butter, diced into half-inch pieces

¼ cup ice-cold water

Granulated sugar, for sprinkling

To make the pastry, combine flour, sugar, and salt. Slowly incorporate butter pieces into the dough, adding ice-cold water until it comes together. Roll into two balls and wrap tightly in plastic wrap. Refrigerate for at least one hour.

To make the filling, combine ¼ cup flour, sugar, and 1 teaspoon of the salt. Add cold diced butter and mix until crumbly.

Combine apples and raisins with the orange or apple juice. Add remaining salt, orange zest, remaining flour, sugar, allspice, cinnamon, and nutmeg, and mix to combine.

Preheat oven to 450 degrees.

Assemble the crostata. From the first ball of chilled dough, roll out into a ¼-inch thick circle. Use your hands to stretch one of the balls of chilled dough into the pie pan, scooching it up a little at the sides of the pan. Spread fruit mixture on top of the dough. From the other ball of dough, pinch off and roll Ping-Pong-sized balls. Stretch the balls into oblong shapes. Place these at random atop the fruit to create a rough, peasant look. Sprinkle all over with sugar.

Bake for about 20 minutes. Serve with homemade whipped cream.

FOR THE FILLING

½ cup flour, divided

⅓ cup sugar

1½ teaspoon sea salt, divided

2 ounces (half a stick) of cold sweet butter, diced

1½ pounds apples (I use McIntosh), cored and cut into chunks (I leave the skins on)

Raisins, a handful

2 tablespoons or so orange or apple juice

1 teaspoon grated orange zest (Lemon or clementine works just as well. Whatever you've got.)

¼ cup flour

⅓ cup sugar

dash of allspice

2 dashes of cinnamon

A little nutmeg

Grandma Lorraine's Cherry Pie with Crunchy Crumb Top

Did I mention my mom was a pie baker? Her pies were known all over St. Louis and southern Illinois. I promise this one will not disappoint. She was not much of a measurer. So I come by it naturally. She used to say, "Ellen, you just need to get the feel of the dough." If you have never made pie dough, you might want to practice by making this dough three or four times. Pretty soon you will get the "feel of the dough," too. I promise.

In the wintertime Mom used Thank You brand pie filling, doctored with a little vanilla, sugar, cinnamon, and a hint of nutmeg, but if you have them you can use seeded bing cherries. (Cut the cherries in half. Mix in a bowl with a little vanilla, sugar, salt, cinnamon, and a hint of nutmeg, and refrigerate for about an hour.)

Mom used to bake these in mini pie tins on the night of the Christmas pageant at church. Every child who was in the play got one. And I was always pretty sure some of the older kids signed up for the pageant year after year just so they could get their pie.

FOR THE CRUST

1½ sticks cold butter, and a bit more for the prepared crust

3 cups flour

1 teaspoon sea salt

1 tablespoon sugar

Cold lard or shortening (Crisco)

½ cup ice water with a little crushed ice

To make the crust, dice butter and put in refrigerator to keep pieces hard and cold. Mix flour, salt, and sugar. Put butter and shortening in food processor and pulse 8 to 10 times until the butter is the size of peas. Pour ice water in and pulse until dough just comes together. Turn dough out onto floured surface and form into two balls. Wrap them separately in plastic wrap. If you're making two uncovered pies, or one covered pie (an alternative to the crumb topping), refrigerate both for at least 30 minutes. If you're only making one uncovered pie, freeze the other ball.

Roll out the chilled dough and fold it in half. Unfold it to fit the pie pan once placed in the pan. Dot the dough with tiny pieces of butter, then add the filling.

Preheat the oven to 450 degrees.

To make the crumb topping, cut the butter into the dry ingredients. Work it together with your hands; you'll have enough for two pies. If you don't use it all, freeze the excess. (You can also toast the topping for 15 minutes at 350 degrees and use on top of fresh fruit, yogurt, or ice cream!)

Once the topping comes together, sprinkle topping over pie filling. Bake pie for 20 minutes and then reduce the temperature to 350 degrees and bake for another 10 to 15 minutes to help set the shape of the crust, so it does not slouch. Watch carefully: You may have to put foil around the crust if it starts to get too dark.

FOR THE FILLING

2 cans cherry pie filling

FOR THE CRUMB TOPPING

1½ sticks sweet butter cut into small pieces

1½ cups flour

3 cups light brown sugar

⅓ cup sugar

½ teaspoon salt

¼ teaspoon cinnamon

Buttermilk Panna Cotta

My best friend in high school was a beautiful Sicilian girl named Francesca. Her family holidays were filled with slow cooking tomato sauce and spicy sazitza. It was very exotic over there. Her house was the first place I ever tasted panna cotta. I could not believe such a good thing existed. I was the kid who licked the cream from the little pitcher on any restaurant table. So to learn there was a dessert dedicated to the glories of cream was like discovering angels. I have made every kind of panna cotta there is, but the simple versions are still the best. You can drizzle a little caramel sauce or even just maple syrup on top. You can also add fruit, but you will not improve it much. It looks a little lonely without any color or topping but it tastes like the purest form of dessert. Creamy, rich, and delicious all at once. This is one of the best tastes there is.

INGREDIENTS

¾ ounce gelatin

Butter for the ramekins

2 whole vanilla beans

1 cup heavy cream

¾ cup sugar

Pinch of good sea salt

2 cups buttermilk

Put gelatin in a small bowl and add water to cover (2 tablespoons or so), stir once, and let stand for a few minutes. Set aside. Butter 8 ramekins. (No ramekins? You can also use wine glasses, tumblers, or coffee cups.)

Split vanilla bean pods and scrape seeds from pods. In a saucepan, combine cream, sugar, salt, and vanilla seeds and pods and cook over medium-low heat for a few minutes, then lower heat. Add gelatin and buttermilk. Remove vanilla pods. Pour mixture into buttered ramekins and let cool for about an hour or until mixture reaches room temperature.

Transfer to refrigerator and chill for about three hours.

Serve with fresh fruit or caramel sauce.

Caramel Sauce

Mix the butter, salt, half-and-half, and brown sugar in a sauté pan and bring to a boil over medium-low heat. Whisk gently for 5 to 7 minutes. Add vanilla and cook one more minute to thicken. Turn off the heat. Pour into a jar and refrigerate or serve warm over panna cotta.

INGREDIENTS

4 tablespoons butter

1 tablespoon salt

½ cup half-and-half

1 cup brown sugar

1 tablespoon vanilla

Pippi

Hannah had just broken up with a boy. She was sad in the way of seventeen-year-old girls throughout all time after a high school romance fades. It was a mopey, lingering kind of sad, and we felt like we needed to do something to change up the narrative.

This girl needed a new love, and there is nothing better than a puppy. The very idea made Hannah giddy. So the research was on. Our friends Ellen and Roger had a Moodle named Milo, who had captured everyone's hearts. Since we already had a Berner and a rowdy Terrier, a little cuddly Moodle seemed like the perfect addition to the pack.

Pippi arrived in our family a few weeks later, and her paws barely touched the floor. When she wasn't in Hannah's arms, she was in Eli's (or mine or John's, truth be told). Right away, we knew that we didn't have just a cuddle girl, though. She was warmly affectionate, all right, but she was also plenty tough. Silvery grizzled Pippi (named for Hannah's favorite childhood literary character) became our Alpha within moments of her arrival. She tugged on 110-pound Eloise's ear to get her to play, and she ran circles around our terrier, Stu. She followed him everywhere, doing whatever he did.

"Corporal Pippi reporting, sir!"

She'd stand sentry next to him, scanning the woods for intruders. She'd run next door to steal pizza crusts for them both from the construction crew working there. Everyone loved Pippi. We love her still.

Chapter Five

Furry Christmas

On Christmas Eve, we shop for the pets. One year we ran into our pal Ellen. Like us, her arms were laden with snowmen and Santa toys. We were buying for our furry gang, and she was buying for hers. Oscar, our Wheaten Terrier, loves red, so the Santa toys are always a hit at our house. There was the usual assortment of bones and chew toys, catnip and fishing poles with feathers on the end. We go on Christmas Eve because these presents don't have to be wrapped. Plus, it's a way to be out and about during the day, when our kids are finally getting around to wrapping presents before the big evening events get rolling.

I like the hustle and bustle of last-minute shopping in Vermont on Christmas Eve. I wouldn't want to have to do it, mind you, but I like being around and in it. People are funny and cheerful. The last-minute shoppers have usually traveled to Vermont to be with family.

And they have been reminded of someone they forgot to buy for. There is the pressure of the last minute, but also the understanding that in an hour or so, what will be will be.

Shopping at the pet store is the very best place to be, though.

"I love these gifts best of all," Ellen said, holding up a squeaky ice-skating penguin in one hand and a collection of peanut butter chews in the other. "Milo is always the most grateful guy on my gift list."

I thought about that. I knew what she meant. Our dogs and kitty, too. It was true gratitude in the deepest sense of the word. They love when we are all together. They like nicking bits of nut roll off the trunk in the library. They roll in the piles of wrapping paper and are absolutely thrilled when a present is passed to them.

Oscar races through the house with his Santa, and Violet, our Bernese Mountain Dog,

prances regally with hers, showing everyone in the room. Olive, Benjamin's Italian Spinone, can never decide. She puts hers down and grabs someone else's in a wild game of Yankee Swap. And Elsie, Hannah's Great Dane, runs after the others with her giant plush reindeer antlers hitting the walls. Even Sadiecat, our Snow Leopard Bengal, gets in on the madcap fun. She always gets the mouse stuffed with some kind of crinkly crunchy plastic wrap that makes satisfying noises when you squeeze it. And she will fetch, too. The fishing pole with the elastic bouncy curling baton is always a hit.

These guys are always happy. They never think we bought the wrong size or color. They don't count to see who has the biggest pile of presents. In a family with a yawning age gap, the youngest human always has the biggest pile. Those toy knights and dragons don't cost much, and unwrapping a multitude is half the fun. There is zero competition amongst the furry family, however, and tons of joy and excitement. No one ever gets mad about "the time that *blah blah blah* happened." These guys completely get Christmas, and they show the rest of us the way.

We even make a big bowl of potatoes for the chickens. My girls love their carbs. With cracked corn and some sweet, slightly stale cookies added to the mix, they are in on the whole Christmas-morning show.

Furry Christmas started for me when I was nine years old. Our two old dogs, Tippy and Snookie (those had not been great naming years), died that year. I'd also had a Siamese cat named Mike (maybe the naming was improving a little by then), but my mom gave him away

because she hated the fur on all her furniture. (I've been quietly rebelling against that with lots of long-living happy animal roommates and fur-covered clothes and furniture ever since.)

I really missed my pets that year. I didn't think it was right to be bereft of them, and you can bet I was not quiet about it, either. I played "How Much Is That Doggie in the Window?" on our old stereo incessantly. I hummed it on Saturday mornings in the car on the way to the beauty shop. Lest my mom missed the hints, I wrote a long letter to Santa on the day after Thanksgiving, and left it pinned to the refrigerator for all the weeks leading up to Christmas. Mom said I could take it to Santa when I went to Famous-Barr with her. But I explained that I'd rather leave the letter out with milk and cookies on Christmas Eve. I didn't even believe in Santa by then, mind you. I had asked about his origins when I was going on six. Still, I trucked him out anytime I needed a little holiday help. This seemed like a Santa emergency, all right.

My sister, Susanne, came to the rescue. She was fifteen years older than I was, and holidays were when she would blow in, like a 1960s glamour-puss showing up for her stage cue. She got in late that Christmas Eve, and immediately said she had an early present for me. My mom (who was in on the secret) told me which one

I could unwrap from underneath the tree. It was a big box filled with doggie paraphernalia. There was a dog bowl, a leash, and some squeaky toys. I looked blank for about a nanosecond and then I looked up at them with a slow expectant grin spreading across my face. Susanne opened the front door and brought him in.

He took my breath right away. Kris (Kringle, of course) was a black standard poodle. He was nearly a year old and the very best present I had ever gotten up to that point. He's still in the top five. He was my best friend for the next seventeen years. He began life with a prim poodle hairdo, transitioned into Rasta dreads with ease, and finally settled into a mature and unsilly coif. He traipsed around with me during my tumultuous teen years and early twenties. He lived in lofts and slept on people's couches with me. He knew every sad thing that had ever happened to me, and he was there celebrating with me when I had my first baby boy.

Kris was stalwart. I loved him fiercely and he loved me back just as hard. And so, at Christmas every year, we celebrated our happy anniversary in a big way. Kris loved soup bones, which my butcher held aside for him. Bone marrow was his favorite, and on Christmas morning he got a giant pile of them. By afternoon,

they were hidden in every nook and cranny of the house.

These days when we bake all of our Christmas goodies, doggy treats are still a favorite part. They are more affordable than store-bought, and all the dogs love them. And besides, I feel like they are rightfully as much a part of the festivities as the rest of us are.

Treats for Four-Legged Friends

Christmas wouldn't be Christmas without celebrating with our furry family. They are as much family as any of the people we are actually related to. Luckily it is just as easy when you are making cookies for your table to mix a batch for the critters at the same time.

And I promise you they will be happy and grateful—Every. Single. Time.

And so . . . for your own Christmasy pet goodies.

Peanut Butter Dog Treats

These are my go-to treats. They whip up fast and the dogs always do those funny little twirls for them.

INGREDIENTS

1½ cups stone-ground whole-wheat flour

1 cup regular flour

½ cup powdered milk

½ cup quick-cooking oatmeal (not instant), plus extra for sprinkling

½ cup smooth peanut butter

2 tablespoons toasted wheat germ

1 extra-large egg, lightly beaten

1 cup water

1 egg beaten with 1 tablespoon water, for egg wash

Preheat the oven to 325 degrees. Line a sheet pan with parchment paper.

In the bowl of an electric mixer fitted with the paddle attachment, combine the two flours, the powdered milk, oatmeal, peanut butter, and wheat germ. With the mixer on low, add the egg and water and mix just until dough forms a slightly sticky ball.

Dump the dough out on a well-floured board and knead it into a ball. Roll the dough out ½-inch thick. Dip a cookie cutter in flour and cut out dog bone shapes . . . you can also cut these freehand. Collect the scraps, knead lightly, roll out again, and cut more dog biscuits.

Place the biscuits on the prepared sheet pan and brush with the egg wash. Sprinkle with oatmeal and bake for 1 hour, until completely hard. Cool and toss to happy dogs.

Minty Fresh Dog Treats

This recipe is great for doggy breath. It uses mint and parsley. They didn't love these as much at first, until I added the cheese. You want a hard, strong cheese here. Don't worry, though, the mint will overpower it on their breath.

INGREDIENTS

1½ cups buckwheat flour (I use Bob's Red Mill)

4 tablespoons fresh parsley, finely chopped

2 tablespoons fresh mint, finely chopped

1 tablespoon pure honey

2 tablespoons olive oil

1 egg, beaten

½ cup strong Parmesan

Water (approximately 1 to 3 teaspoons)

Preheat oven to 400 degrees.

In a large bowl, stir together buckwheat flour, parsley, and mint leaves until combined.

In a small bowl, whisk together honey and olive oil. Pour honey and olive oil mixture into the flour mixture and stir. Add egg and cheese and stir until well combined.

Knead dough with hands to thoroughly mix the ingredients together. Add a little bit of water at a time till the dough comes together. This should take a few minutes.

Using a rolling pin, roll the dough out to approx. ¼-inch thick. Cut into desired shapes with cookie dough cutter. Place biscuits onto a nonstick baking sheet and bake for 15 minutes.

Store these biscuits in an airtight container in the fridge.

Apple Cheddar Dog Treats

Our pups appreciate variety in their snack foods just like we do. Apple Cheddar is a favorite. Confession: I always taste the batter and it tastes as good to me as cookie batter does. I like knowing what they are eating. Anyway, barley flour is the key.

Preheat oven to 350 degrees. Line a baking sheet with parchment paper.

In a large bowl, mix together all ingredients to form the dough. Wrap dough in plastic and chill for a couple of hours.

Roll out mixture to ¼-inch thick and cut out biscuits with a 3½-inch bone or paw-print cookie cutter. Reroll scraps and continue cutting out biscuits.

Space biscuits 1 inch apart on prepared baking sheet. Bake for 30 minutes until nicely browned and firm.

Transfer biscuits to a wire rack. Turn off oven and place biscuits on wire rack in oven overnight. Remove from oven and store up to 2 weeks.

INGREDIENTS

2 cups barley flour

½ cup old-fashioned oatmeal

⅓ cup shredded cheddar

¼ cup grated Parmesan

⅓ cup unsweetened applesauce

2 tablespoons olive oil

3 tablespoons water

Pupsicles

Pupsicles are fast treats. They don't last long. But our furry family loves them so much that I make them over and over.

Combine all ingredients in a blender. Blend until smooth. Pour into ice-cube trays or small bowls. Freeze until solid.

These are best eaten outside or on the porch.

INGREDIENTS

¼ cup peanut butter

½ cup plain yogurt

1 ripe banana

1 teaspoon ground flax seed (optional)

Splash of unsweetened almond milk

Deviled Eggs

I am known for my deviled eggs. People love them. They actually ask about them ahead of parties. Over the years, I have decided that this is not a terrible reputation to have. It might be better to be known for your famous fancy soufflé. But there is a sweet comfort, too, in being the woman who can be counted on to turn out something reliable and delicious.

I think it goes back to that Facebook question: If you only had twenty-four hours left on earth, what would you do with your day? The first thing I would do is make a batch of good deviled eggs.

A friend from Virginia calls mine Yankee deviled eggs, because they are sweet, which is, as far as he is concerned, not quite right. Although, can I just say? He eats them by the handful.

People are always asking what makes them sweet, as if I have some secret spice or special trick. I do. It's called sugar. Sugar gets a bad rap as far as I am concerned. I love it. This is not corn syrup. It isn't fructose. Or red dye No. 5. It isn't honey or agave either. Plain old-fashioned sugar. It sweetens in the most delightful and, yes, unexpected ways.

I make all kinds of deviled eggs. Sometimes I make them with bits of pancetta and scallions for a bacon-and-eggs experience. At a fancier party, I might add lemon and basil or smoked salmon and dill, which gives them a lovely pink color. I have even made them with lobster for a really decadent egg.

Deviled eggs meet all my requirements. They are fast, easy, and delicious. Some people like elaborate party food that takes hours to prepare. Food that stands up tall on the plate like a little sculpture. I can appreciate that food. But it is not for me. I just like my food to taste good.

This little ornament, a gift from my Hannah, has become a favorite. It seems to say, "Look. It worked. Your daughter gets it, too. Christmas will continue. Because, by golly, this thing is your legacy."

Chapter Six

Uncle Felix

It was the year of the firetruck. Benjamin was about five and he loved all things firefighting that year. Firefighters and firetrucks. Sirens and red. We had found the perfect Christmas present for a boy whose conversation was on the All-Firetruck Channel. It was one of those little motorized cars that he could actually drive. It had a hose and ladder, flashing light and a siren. It went about three miles an hour and we just knew he was going to love it.

The package came about two weeks before Christmas and was promptly hidden in our bedroom closet underneath a pile of pillows and blankets. I would lift them up for a look every morning when I got dressed, and I would grin. I could hardly wait.

John found a great fireman's helmet. It was a real old helmet that the fire department wasn't using anymore. We got him a slicker that looked pretty authentic, too. We were pretty excited parents.

Christmas Eve that year was perfect. We had gone to Aunt Mindy's for Christmas Eve breakfast. Then we'd gone to John's grandma's in the afternoon and celebrated with his family. My mom's for Christmas Eve supper. When we left her house, we told Benjamin and Hannah, then almost two, that we had to hurry home so we could all get to sleep so Santa could come.

Then, practically the best thing ever happened. We passed a cornfield filled with deer. In the moonlight, they looked just like reindeer stopping for a snack, so we paused, giggled, then raced home so we could beat Santa.

Those kids were happy to get ready for bed. We'd left the Santa letters on the table next to the cookies and milk, with carrots for the reindeer. We tucked Benjamin and Hannah in, reading *The Star of Melvin* and *Jolly Old Santa Claus* one more time. Then the grown-ups headed downstairs to get the presents under the tree.

John had a surprise waiting for me. He'd discovered that year that I'd never seen the old Barbara Stanwyck movie *Christmas in Connecticut*. He'd planned a romantic evening for us. There was a bottle of port, a hunk of cheese, and the movie to savor. I could not believe how much I loved that movie. It was made for me. We watched it and imagined living on a farm in New England. The idea of a romantic sleigh ride pretty much sold us on the eventual move right then. It would be a bunch more years before we finally figured out how to make it happen, but the seed was planted next to our Christmas tree with Uncle Felix and Elizabeth, the film's wily coconspirators, that very night. It was the absolute perfect movie for two people in love with each other, with Christmas, and with the idea of a country life. It is still just about my favorite movie of all time. And there aren't too many Christmas Eves around here that do not include it.

Every year, John makes the fire, I make the popcorn, and we snuggle up. We know all the lines and can recite them practically in harmony. It doesn't matter. We watch that sleigh ride and feel glad and grateful.

Truly, and this may be a little bit of blasphemy, but I sort of think movies, TV specials, and books are as much about the Christmas spirit as church on Christmas Eve. ABC Family channel has something they call the 25 Days of Christmas. I'll bet families all over America watch those shows just like we did when our kids were little. But now with Netflix and smart TVs, it is possible to curate the holiday offerings in very specific ways.

These movies and TV shows are sweet, shared, cultural memories that have the power to entertain, to teach, to soothe, and to bake in tradition. *A Charlie Brown Christmas* was a mainstay of my own childhood experience, and I wanted to make sure our kids had some of those same sweet memories. Just the sound of Schroeder on that little piano puts me in the mood for Christmas. Those Peanuts skaters are an American tradition that says slow down, get in touch with the little kid in you who loves a good snow day. Eat the damn cookie.

Of course, we also have favorite Christmas books, too. With the annual marathon showings of *A Christmas Story,* lots of people know Jean Shepherd's story. The book is also a treasure. We love it around here.

Our first Christmas, I gave John Truman

Capote's *A Christmas Memory,* and we have read it together every year since. We have a long list of favorite books including *Jolly Old Santa Claus,* which was a childhood favorite. Do you know this one? Mary Jane Tonn's story of Santa's workshop? It's illustrated by George Hinke, a classically trained German painter. He illustrated for *Ideals* in the 1940s and '50s. His paintings of Santa and Mrs. Claus, Whiskers the Cat, and all the Elves (called Brownies) delighted me and every child I have ever known. Who am I kidding? They still delight me. It is worth looking up an old copy of this one from the '50s. The reissues are not nearly as rich as the original was. I promise you, it will become a family treasure. Ours gets trucked out every year for any child who shows up at our house during any time remotely close to Christmas.

These stories are the backdrop. The day you take the day off and have cocoa and oatmeal for breakfast while watching *Frosty the Snowman* will be the day you decide to keep it in the routine next year. I am dying for some little grandbabies so I can repeat the whole happy mess.

Christmas wouldn't be Christmas for us without these stories. And because a Vermont winter is long, it pays to start early and make them last.

All this to say that Barbara Stanwyck was a great way to get us ready for putting out the presents. We finished our winter wine and the movie and started placing the presents under the tree. John carried down the big box with the firetruck inside. We were both in for another surprise.

When we opened the box we discovered a firetruck, all right. Or the idea of a firetruck, anyway. It was red, and in about two hundred pieces. With directions and maps. In a foreign language. Okay, that part really isn't true. But it might as well have been, given how mechanically uninclined the two of us are.

It had been a giant box. We'd assumed a put-together firetruck would emerge from it. Only, of course it didn't. We sobered up fast and started looking for screwdrivers and better light. The directions were unfathomable by Christmas-tree light but maybe with more wattage?

John took the whole kit and caboodle out to the mudroom in case anyone should wander down and catch this midnight elf. I put some carols on the stereo and kept the coffee coming. Truthfully, I may have dozed on the couch. Finally, somewhere around 1:00 A.M., he had a eureka moment and it came together quickly after that. Then the real trouble started.

The truck was bigger than it had looked in

a box in the closet. Way bigger. It sat gleaming and gorgeous in the mudroom, but it would not fit through the doorway back into the house. It wouldn't go through the outside door either. The door panels had to come back off and the whole thing had to be reassembled under the tree.

We were both exhausted when we finally climbed the steps at 3:00 A.M. The kids woke up in what seemed like fifteen minutes after we went to bed.

Worth it, though. The firetruck was every bit the hit we had imagined it would be. There were giant smiles and squeals and Benjamin carried little Hannah on his lap as he saved her from countless deadly fires all day long. Hannah had gotten a play kitchen that year, and she kept the firefighter supplied in tea and pancakes in between being saved from terrible restaurant fires.

The Christmas Eves of the early years are busier than the ones that are coming. Young parents carry all the freight of making memories during what are often the leanest years of a family just starting out. Leanest in every sense of the word. You are literally living on the skinny. Sleep deprivation is typical. And there are the pressures of family traditions on all sides. Merging those cultures can seem like a job for the UN.

I think those may be the years when the fan-

tasy of Christmas often gets lost in the grind of it. There are books, and even workshops, now on how to minimize holiday stress. That matters, too. It makes good sense to figure out what you love about the holidays, and get more of that. And get a lot less of the parts that feel like a burden.

For example, I love getting Christmas cards. I even like buying them, and imagining reconnecting with far-flung friends. But I do not enjoy writing them. It is a chore that I put off, and in the years when it eventually gets done I begrudge the time I spend on them. My handwriting is awful, so my wrists ache from the pressure of trying to make little pithy notes legible. It is no fun.

One year when I realized I was dreading it, I just quit. I took the expensive beautiful boxes of cards over to the post office and left them on the counter for someone else. There are probably people who love writing them. Those are the people who should be sending them. I don't get as many as I used to now, since some folks cut you from their lists when they don't get one back. And I miss those that have gone. But not as much as I dreaded writing my own.

The trick to Christmas, it seems to me, is making it your own. Not your mother's, not the one the magazines are selling this year, but the one you actually long to have. Cut obligations ruthlessly and only add activities that are fun and meaningful to you and your family. Protect your traditions as zealously as you guard your kids at the pool, and Christmas will come true.

Here's what I know for sure. Those early years will pass in a blur. It is trite but true that babies become children, children kids, and teenagers adults, in such fast succession that one day you will look at photographs and wonder at your impossible youth. I don't think anyone ever regrets the years they missed sleep on Christmas Eve or the day they all stayed home in their jammies and watched Christmas cartoons all day. I can also promise you the work you missed, or the holiday parties you skipped, will not haunt you. Listening to your kids tell a college friend about the year of the firetruck, though . . . that will never ever get old.

And if you'd like a few recommendations for books and movies to relish every Christmas, give these a try. Maybe you'll find a new one to add to your own list. Here are snacks perfect for movie watching, too. Fast, simple, and delicious. Good words for a busy season.

Movies

The Shop Around the Corner (1940, I promise you'll like it)
Christmas in Connecticut (1945)
It's a Wonderful Life (1946)
Miracle on 34th Street (the original 1947 version, of course)
The Bishop's Wife (1947 was a good year)

Rudolph the Red Nosed Reindeer (1964)
A Charlie Brown Christmas (1965)
The Night the Animals Talked (1970)
A Christmas Story (1983)
The Santa Clause (1994)

Books

FOR EVERYONE . . .

A Christmas Carol, by Charles Dickens
(Always a wonderful, if obvious, choice.
At least every couple of years.)
A Christmas Story, by Jean Shepherd
Jolly Old Santa Claus, by Mary Jane Tonn
(Forget that this looks like a kid's book.
You will love it too. I promise.)

FOR KIDS . . .

Auntie Claus, by Elise Primavera
Fat Santa, by Margery Cuyler and Marsha
Winborn
The Mitten, by Jan Brett
The Star of Melvin, by Nathan Zimelman

FOR THE GROWN-UPS . . .

A Christmas Memory, by Truman Capote
Esther's Gift, by Jan Karon
Holidays on Ice, by David Sedaris

Movie Night

It used to be that we had to wait for the one night a year when Charlie Brown dragged that little bedraggled tree back to his friends and showed us all the true meaning of Christmas. But these days with smart TVs and streaming and all the rest, you can plan your Christmas movie nights on the days that work best for you. Might as well plan some yummy treats at the same time.

Maple Bacon Popcorn

Life is too short not to take the five minutes required to make real popcorn. The microwave and fake butter have not improved on the original. You want to hear the sounds of those kernels popping. You are aiming for that wonderful *ping* as they hit the side of your old metal pan that you keep just for popcorn. You can use a little neutral oil like grape seed and get popcorn that tastes like real honest corn. Then when you add a little sea salt and real butter you will be seven years old again watching the giant dinosaur at the drive-in. Popcorn has staying power for a reason. This recipe does do one thing new. It makes old reliable movie popcorn festive and holiday-ready.

INGREDIENTS

- 1 tablespoon oil (I use grape seed because it is virtually flavorless)
- ⅓ cup popcorn kernels
- ½ cup chopped crispy bacon (6 strips)
- ½ cup pure maple syrup (I use B grade)
- ¼ cup (½ stick) sweet butter
- 2 tablespoons bourbon (I use Buffalo Trace but I doubt if it matters)
- 1½ teaspoons flaky sea salt (I use Maldon)

Heat oil in a heavy-bottomed pan over medium heat. (You can use grape seed, canola, vegetable, etc., but not olive oil, it is too likely to burn.)

Add a few popcorn kernels to the pan, cover, and let it heat up. When one kernel pops, add ⅓ cup of uncooked popcorn kernels and cover the pan. Shake the pan a little to spread the kernels in an even layer. Let the kernels pop for several minutes until the pan is full and the popping slows down. Remove from heat and transfer popcorn to a large bowl.

Preheat the oven to 250 degrees. Line a 10 x 15-inch baking sheet with parchment paper. When the popcorn is popped, spread into a single layer on the baking sheet. Disperse the chopped bacon on top of the popcorn. Set aside.

In a heavy-bottomed saucepot over medium-low heat, melt the maple syrup and butter together. Bring to a simmer, and continue to cook for 2 to 3 minutes, then remove from heat and stir in the

bourbon and sea salt. Pour over the popcorn-bacon mixture and stir
to evenly distribute the syrup mixture.

　　Bake for 35 to 40 minutes, stirring frequently, until very fragrant
and the syrup has started to harden. Remove from the oven and
immediately toss. Transfer to a parchment-lined platter and break
up any large pieces.

Prosciutto Fig Mascarpone Flatbread

Sometimes on movie night we have intermission. In theory, intermission is when you walk outside with the dogs, tuck the chickens in for the night, and close their little red door. The chicken house is only about fifty yards from our house, but when we come back in, we say the same thing every single time. "I kinda worked up an appetite out there. Wanna share another pizza?" Like maybe it's a novel idea. Really we were saving up all along for this one.

I often buy fresh figs at Christmas and fill them with Gorgonzola and tiny bits of walnut for an elegant, easy party food. But it's hard to find fresh figs in the wintertime, so I have to order a whole case from the little Italian market in the village. That's a lot of figs. This was what I figured out to do with the rest of them. (When you can't get fresh figs, the jam works almost as well.)

First you get the crunch of the charred crust, then comes the creamy mascarpone just ahead of the salty prosciutto, with a fast hit of sugar from the sweetness of the figs. When people taste this for the first time they get a sort of thoughtful, faraway look on their faces. Then there's the slow smile. Same routine. Every time.

Dough makes two 10-inch flatbreads

continued on next page

Pea Garlic Mascarpone Galette

We were starving. So that was bad. But we were in Italy, which of course was very, very good. On this day, we were wandering around Florence at that odd time of day when all the restaurants have closed from lunch and none have opened up again for supper. We finally spotted this family café that had a big boisterous party left over from lunch. We sidled in and before you knew it the servers were bringing us the same piles of food they were still bringing them. This galette was the first bite I took that day. The cheese was runny and the peas were fresh. The crust was thin and floury and a little burnt and we have been re-creating it on movie night ever since.

Dough makes two 10-inch flatbreads

FOR THE DOUGH

2   cups flour (all-purpose or bread flour)

1   package rapid-rise yeast (do not proof)

½   teaspoon salt

⅔   cup warm water

Olive oil

Cornmeal

FOR THE TOP

Mascarpone

Garlic powder

1   bag frozen peas

Parmesan

For the dough, mix together flour, yeast, and salt and then slowly incorporate the water. Use your stand mixer with hook attachment and work the dough for 5 to 10 minutes until it is a nice elastic ball. If you don't have a mixer, you can easily knead by hand. Add more warm water or flour if dough is too sticky or lacks elasticity.

Place ball in a bowl greased with a little bit of olive oil and flip it over so both sides are oiled. Cover and let rest in a warm draft-free area.

Preheat oven to 500 degrees. When dough has doubled in size, punch the dough down on a floured surface. If you have a pizza stone, place in hot oven. If you don't have a stone, use a cookie sheet.

Roll out the dough. Toss it in the air to help thin it out. Keep stretching. Brush the top with olive oil. Sprinkle a tiny amount of cornmeal on wooden paddle. Use paddle to put dough in the oven. Bake for 2 minutes until it is lightly golden. Pull it out and put the second dough in the oven.

Toppings: Lightly smear mascarpone on the dough, mostly on the edges. Sprinkle garlic powder and then frozen peas. Sprinkle finely grated Parmesan. Bake a few minutes until beautiful and gold.

Let it cool before slicing. Serve with freshly ground sea salt on top.

The Rule

There was the year we almost didn't find our ornaments. We were in New York City. The first stop was a very fancy shop in the Village. I was just sure one of us was going to break something and come away with a bill for a thousand dollars. The spun glass ornaments looked like they had been shipped in that day from an ancient glassblower in the Czech Republic. Beautiful, but fragile looking. The owner did not seem to appreciate our booming little family.

We moved on to a Christmas shop at the Pier at South Street Seaport. That place felt like Christmas Anywhere USA. They had cloth Santas, snow globes, music boxes playing "The Little Drummer Boy." There was, also, a talking snowman whose hat had slipped. His voice seemed a little sluggish, as if his battery was running out.

This had never happened to us before. We were used to hitting it out of the park on the first try. We were heading back to our hotel for a reviving hot cocoa when we were captivated along the way by a shop window. The display was a blue-and-white wintery wonderland with cabins and wood smoke, forest animals and snow.

We all steered straight for the door in silent agreement and were soon lost among the trees and the magic. As I've mentioned, Eli likes his ornaments big and sugary, and his hand went right to the biggest, brightest, most ornamental-iest ornament in the place. It was a giant spun-glass ball with a dozen bright colors swirled in. He grabbed for it and could barely hold it in both his hands.

We got him a basket and filled it with tissue paper so he could carry his precious cargo safely. But then as we were checking out, he wailed. He'd seen another one, a better one. This version had a concave section with mirrored colors inside. It was an even louder version of Ornament Number One. But, you know, there's The Rule: One ornament per person.

Thirty minutes of going back and forth, and then Benjamin offered, "I'll give up mine so he can have two."

Sweet, but what about the tradition? Besides, Eli's two ornaments cost more than all the rest of ours combined. What was I thinking? I don't know. We'd already made an exception to The Rule one year to save a mopey teenager . . . now what? Maybe I figured that it wouldn't be special if we

didn't have to make choices. But then Eli came up with a solution.

He had a stash of money he'd brought along for souvenirs. He had saved $137 and was carrying it in a thick wad in his pocket. Why couldn't this be his souvenir? Why, indeed? We bought him one, and he bought the other. Good rules, after all, are like good recipes. They are mostly just guides. And every time I look at my tree, I remember that day, and I feel glad all over again. Because that ornament was way more than just an ornament. They all are.

Chapter Seven

Fa~La~La~ing

We hadn't been in Vermont very long when it was time for our twentieth annual Christmas party. The guest list had changed over the years, as guest lists tend to do. But now that we'd moved a thousand miles away, most of the list had turned over. There might have been different people, but the themes stayed the same.

First, there is always lots of bad-for-you but delicious party food. No vegetable platters here. I might feel smug while peeling and cutting a big pile of carrots, but they always wind up in the chicken yard the next day. Ours is a festival of debauchery.

Every year, there are tenderloin sandwiches with balsamic onions and Gorgonzola. Sometimes they are nestled against potato boats and beside trays of oysters. A truly decadent mac 'n' cheese makes an appearance more years than not (page 88).

There might possibly be a little fruit, but it would be accompanied by a dip made from cream cheese and Fluff, so it certainly wouldn't count as healthy, either. And there is always a

who you saw smooching whom, and eat leftover tenderloin with the good sea salt while standing at the counter. The morning after is quite often the best part. The flowers are still beautiful, and if you planned it right you have some good eggy brioche ready to serve. Mugs of steaming coffee and everyone talking around the table in their jammies will be the party you will remember.

Party Foods

Don't you love when you go to someone else's house for a party and they greet you with a hug and a smile and hand you a lovely drink right after you walk in the door? People will remember you and your party forever if you just make delicious foods that actually taste good. Here are some reliable ones. Now please don't forget the music!

Yankee Deviled Eggs

If you have to be known for a recipe, the humble deviled egg is not a bad way to go. You can make these fancy or plain. Folks will eat them at breakfast or with barbecue. You can add caviar or pickles. They can be thick or creamy. Sweet or savory. The deviled egg tells you more about the cook and her mood on that day and in that one moment than practically any other food. If I can whip up a batch of deviled eggs I figure I can solve practically anything that needs solving.

INGREDIENTS

12 eggs

3 tablespoons mayonnaise

2 tablespoons plain yellow mustard

4 tablespoons butter, optional; this gives you a creamier filling

Dash of lemon juice

2 to 3 minced scallions (whites and greens)

A handful of sugar, about 2 tablespoons to taste (This is what makes them Yankee!)

Hard-boil the eggs (If you have your own chickens, use older eggs, because they peel easier. If you get your eggs from the grocery store, they are likely old enough.) Peel and cut in half length-wise. Remove and whip yolks.

In a separate bowl, combine mayonnaise, mustard, butter, if using, lemon juice, scallions, and sugar, and make a paste, slowly adding to yolks until you reach desired consistency. Spoon yolk mixture into egg whites.

Variations: A barely crisped pancetta makes a good bacon-and-egg dish. Salmon and dill in place of the scallions makes for barely pink, delicious eggs. Use basil in place of scallions for another great variation. Diced lobster tail with extra lemon is a really decadent choice.

Coffee Cream Puffs

These are delicate. They will remind you of the offerings at the doughnut shop when you were little, only all dolled up for shiny grown-up life. They have a sophisticated taste and look gorgeous on the cookie platter. People will swoon.

Okay, this one is not difficult but there are a few steps.

Preheat the oven to 375 degrees.

In a saucepan, combine milk, water, butter, sugar, and salt, and bring to a low boil over soft heat. Remove from the heat and add the flour. Mix until dough is smooth. Return to the heat for a minute to dry the dough a bit, then add the eggs, one at a time, and mix until the dough is smooth.

Pipe mounds of dough the size of golf balls onto a parchment-lined sheet. I use a plastic baggie for this step, but you can also buy something called a piping bag with a large tip. I smooth and round the tops of the mounds with a teaspoon dipped in water.

Bake for 15 minutes, then reduce the heat to 325 and bake another 10 minutes. (Reducing the heat allows puffs to dry out on the inside a bit more, without adding too much color.)

Meanwhile, make the coffee cream. Combine cornstarch, flour, and the ½ cup of sugar. Add the yolks and ¼ cup of the milk. Whisk together. Separately, bring remaining milk and the vanilla bean and seeds to a slow boil. Strain bean and seeds from the hot milk, then pour milk slowly into the egg mixture, whisking fast so it doesn't curdle. Put mixture back on low heat, whisking constantly until it thickens. Once it's thick, take off heat and add coffee and butter.

Cover cream with tight plastic wrap and refrigerate for a few hours until it is cold and thick enough to pipe. Make a slit in the base of each puff and pipe cream in. Then dust puffs all over with the powdered sugar.

FOR THE PUFFS

½ cup whole milk

½ cup water

7 tablespoons sweet butter

1½ teaspoons sugar

¼ teaspoon salt

1 cup flour

4 large eggs

Powdered sugar for dusting

FOR THE CREAM

2 tablespoons cornstarch

¼ cup flour

½ cup plus 2 tablespoons sugar

4 egg yolks

2 cups whole milk

1 vanilla bean, split, seeds scraped out and seeds and bean reserved

4 teaspoons instant coffee granules

2 tablespoons sweet butter, cut into tiny cubes

Spicy Pecans

Some people say they don't like sweet nuts. Others ask if the nuts are spicy and then say they don't like those. Here's what I do. I tell the no-spicy people they are sweet and the no-sweet people they are spicy. Both things are true. And everybody's happy. I always run out.

INGREDIENTS

1 teaspoon kosher salt

½ teaspoon ground cumin

½ teaspoon cayenne pepper

½ teaspoon ground cinnamon

½ teaspoon dried ground orange peel

1 pound pecan halves

4 tablespoons sweet butter

¼ cup packed light brown sugar

2 tablespoons packed dark brown sugar

2 tablespoons water

Line a half sheet pan with parchment paper and set aside. Mix the salt, cumin, cayenne, cinnamon, and orange peel together in a small bowl and set aside.

Place the nuts in a 10-inch cast-iron skillet and set over medium heat. Cook, stirring frequently, for 4 to 5 minutes until nuts just start to brown and smell toasted. Add the butter and stir until it melts. Add the spice mixture and stir to combine. Once combined, add light brown and dark brown sugar and water, stirring until the mixture thickens and coats the nuts, approximately 2 to 3 minutes.

Transfer the nuts to the prepared sheet pan, and separate them with a fork or spatula. Allow the nuts to cool completely before transferring to an airtight container for storage. Can be stored up to 3 weeks.

Aunt Loraine's Brady Bunch Cheese Ball

I am a cheese snob. Give me a good strong Taleggio or a rich, creamy blue and I will serve it alongside a fruit-forward Beaujolais with salty oily almonds and a little fig and be happy all the livelong day. This cheese ball does not look like something a real cheese person would want to eat. I know. Trust me. Make it anyway.

INGREDIENTS

3 cups grated extra-sharp cheddar

8 ounces cream cheese

2 tablespoons mayonnaise

⅓ cup chopped green olives

3 teaspoons Worcestershire sauce

2 dashes garlic powder

4 dashes celery seed

¼ teaspoon black pepper

12 ounces chopped pecans

Mix up all the ingredients except for the pecans and form into a ball, then cover the ball with the pecans. Wrap in plastic wrap and place in the refrigerator so the ball can chill and solidify and flavors blend (a couple of hours).

Serve with Ritz Crackers for a festive retro vibe.

Candied Bacon-Wrapped Water Chestnuts

Bacon is the easiest way I know to please a crowd. There is something about the smell and sizzle of bacon. It reminds us all of our moms and dads in the kitchen on Saturday morning. Here you get the sweet and smoke of the bacon and the crunch of the water chestnut in what is practically a perfect party bite. They are much less expensive than the kind with the scallops, and you run way less risk of winding up with something with too chewy a center.

INGREDIENTS

1   cup ketchup

1   cup brown sugar

1   teaspoon
    Worcestershire sauce

2   (8 ounce) cans water
    chestnuts, drained

16 ounces sliced bacon

Preheat oven to 350.

Combine ketchup, brown sugar, and Worcestershire sauce in a saucepan and warm gently until just about boiling. Cut bacon slices into thirds. Cut some of the bigger water chestnuts in half. Wrap chestnuts in bacon and secure with toothpicks. Place in a 9 x 13-inch baking dish. Pour sauce over bacon and water chestnuts. Bake until bacon is completely cooked, about 45 to 50 minutes.

Fried Oysters with Homemade Tartar Sauce

There is never anything wrong with a fried oyster. Plus, they are fast but seem extravagant. Our friend Aaron Zeender, a famed Martha's Vineyard chef, whipped a bunch of these up for us one Thanksgiving when we were all cooking and feeling hungry but still too far from the finish line. It was the perfect pick-me-up. I have been throwing them together at holidays ever since when we are all tired and in need of a little lift.

You want an oyster that feels like it was wrapped in cracklin'. The key is lots of seasoning in a thin batter. For seasoning, Peltier's Rub works a trick (see entry for Brockton Spice Company, Appendix II, New England Flavors). I'll bet some tiny bits of pancetta would be good too. Once I added pistachios, but it was almost too much. Maybe if they had been finer . . .

Serve with homemade tartar sauce, aka remoulade.

Fill a bowl with buttermilk and soak the oysters for about an hour. In a separate bowl, add flour, steak seasoning, and a sprinkle of cornmeal.

Roll the oysters (wet but not drippy) one at a time in the flour mixture and fry a few at a time. Get the pan hot (heavy stock pot or deep-fry pan), add oil, and heat it to 375 degrees. Drop the oysters in until they are golden brown. They will curl a little when they are done. It happens very fast, about a minute. Drain them on a brown-paper-bag-lined plate.

INGREDIENTS

Buttermilk

2 dozen small-sized oysters, shucked

½ cup flour (00 flour works best, extra fine, most refined grade)

1 teaspoon steak seasoning (or use a creole seasoning if you want a spicier taste)

Sprinkle of fine cornmeal

2 inches peanut oil (or grape seed oil)

Homemade Tartar Sauce

Depending on where you live, you may call this yummy sauce tartar sauce or remoulade. Some folks say it's the raw eggs in the mayo that make it one and not the other. Others say it is whether or not you use anchovies. I say both practically interchangeably. Call it whatever you want. It's good.

INGREDIENTS

1 cup mayonnaise (Homemade mayo is so much better than store-bought. It might take you a couple of times to get a feel for it. The recipe follows. Otherwise, open a jar.)

Thinly sliced garlic

½ cup minced green onion

Handful of capers

½ cup chopped dill pickles

1 to 2 tablespoons hot sauce

1 tablespoon honey (or to taste)

Bunch of fresh tarragon, finely chopped without stems

Dash of cayenne

Salt, to taste

A little mustard (dry or prepared), optional

Whisk all ingredients until well combined, then chill.

Homemade Mayonnaise

Whisk all ingredients save the oil. Then gradually add ¼ cup of the oil, a dot at a time. Literally a dot at a time for about 4 minutes, whisking hard and constantly. Add remaining oil in a slow stream, whisking constantly. Chill.

INGREDIENTS

1 large egg

2 teaspoons lemon juice

2 teaspoons white wine or champagne vinegar

¼ teaspoon Dijon mustard

Salt

¾ cup olive oil

Onion Bacon Tart

I like mine "rustic." This means I don't roll out the dough in a perfectly even square or make perfect edges. Language can be as important to the meal as the food is.

Makes 1 tart

INGREDIENTS

3 tablespoons olive oil

2 tablespoons sweet butter

3½ ounces lardons or diced bacon

1 pound onions, thinly sliced

Sea salt and pepper

1 tablespoon honey

1 tablespoon really good balsamic

1 bunch fresh tarragon

1 sheet puff pastry

Flour for rolling out

Heat olive oil, butter, and bacon and cook until the bacon browns, then add the onions and salt and pepper and cook until the onions are golden brown. Add honey, balsamic, and tarragon. Increase heat to high to reduce liquid. Turn off heat and set aside to cool.

Preheat oven to 350 degrees.

Roll puff pastry out on lightly floured surface and form into pastry shell. Scoop onion and bacon mixture into pastry shell and bake until crisp and golden.

Kitty in a Stocking

It started one Thanksgiving after we'd been reading stories about turkeys. Our little girl was curious about the connection between turkeys in the storybooks and turkeys on the Thanksgiving Day table. It wasn't long before our soon-to-be-former carnivore was asking us where beef came from. The day she asked about sausage, I saw the sad disapproval in her eyes when she said, "Oh, Mommy, not piggies." Our Hannah became a lifelong vegetarian when she was just five.

So it is no surprise that the ornaments she chooses tend to be animals, starting with the Kitty in a Stocking when she was three. We'd had a run of business that year, which had not included a spay trip to the vet. So we had brought two—count 'em! two—litters of adorable kittens into the world. We'd kept a couple of the kitties and diligently found homes for all the rest.

Hannah had mothered those babies and put them in her little Fisher-Price shopping cart with blankets and pillows and walked them all over the neighborhood. These were some very well socialized kittens. We were on Adventure weekend when she spied the little Kitty in a Stocking ornament. It was an adorable, if obvious, choice. She carried it in her little fist all weekend long, and Kitty has held a place of honor on our tree ever since.

Except for the year we lost her, when Hannah was twenty-four but with the same sweet innocence she'd had the year Kitty was acquired.

We went through all the tubs and unwrapped every piece of tissue paper there was. We searched. Hannah was worried. Finally, John wondered if maybe we had accidentally left her on the tree the year before. We take our old trees out to the woods, where local chipmunks can burrow inside, giving the trees a new kind of glow and warmth. So there was some possibility that Kitty had been missed and carted out over the hills and through the woods along with the tree. She could be anywhere.

John bundled up in minus-seven-degree weather and traipsed right out to the woods, where last year's tree was fading fast. Digging through branches and pulling aside little nests, he found her.

Well, of course he did.

Kitty was tucked deep inside an old branch where a tiny family of mice was scrunched up. Not only did he retrieve Kitty, he came home, grabbed a load of dryer lint, and went back out to tuck it around the mice.

'Cause that, after all, is the guy I married. Ornament finder and protector of mouse babies. It's a good combination.

Chapter Eight

'Twas the Night

John talks about his childhood Christmas Eve at his grandmother's as the best night of the year. He had several aunts and uncles and a whole slew of cousins, but they were all far away. So on Christmas Eve it was just his family at Grandma's. The table was laden with all of her favorite old-world foods from Czechoslovakia. John remembers starving himself all day so he would have room for it all.

His grandmother's presents for him were under her tree. It's funny, but for a long time when he talked about these big celebrations, with music and dancing and food, I always imagined his aunts and uncles and cousins in the mix. It wasn't until we had been married for a whole quarter of a century that I learned that by the time he came along (he was the youngest), it was just his family and Grandma. The

stories of our childhood loom so large in our memories that the "facts" often don't describe the experiences very well.

My own childhood Christmas Eves were often at my Aunt Loraine and Uncle Louie's house. My dad died when I was just five years old, and his sister kept inviting us for the holidays so that we could be with that side of the family. My mom had two brothers who spent Christmas Eve with their wives' families.

Note to self and all moms of boys: This happens a lot. So we all better make friends with those sweet daughters-in-law and be flexible enough to grab holidays on whatever dates work for everyone.

Aunt Loraine and Uncle Louie always gave the very best Christmas presents. They would think up stuff I had no idea I wanted but would love for years. They were responsible for the

woodburning kit one year and the Easy-Bake Oven another. I made little coasters with flowers on them with that woodburning kit and cupcakes with the oven. I can still smell the creosote coming off the wood and touch the old scar I have on my hand from all the burns I racked up.

I would be excited all day, wondering what might be under the tree for me that year. As an added bonus, my Aunt Loraine made a delicious cheese ball that seemed somehow exotic to me (page 170). I still make it. I don't care if it looks like it came straight from a *Brady Bunch* Christmas special. It tasted good then, and it still does.

All day long my mother and I would bake more cookies to replace the ones we had already given away or eaten ourselves. We'd make her famous Christmas boots (aka stockings). These were felt projects with glitter and bells. Since there always seemed to be someone coming to Christmas who didn't have one yet, we made them year after year. My job was to sew the little glitter circles onto the felt Christmas trees that took center stage on each boot. It was an important job and I took it seriously.

We wrapped presents and sang along with Bing and Nat, Ella and Dean, eating cookies all day and getting a good sugar high going into the event. My mom and my aunt shared a name, which might seem a little confusing to folks not in the family. They were Lorraine and Loraine. But you can bet that there was more than one r separating them. The Lor(r)aines were both important to me, growing up. And one thing about the Lor(r)aines, they were both charter members of the beauty shop and they *got* Christmas.

Eventually everybody grows up and we get to build our own family Christmas memories. We developed ours special up here in the North Country. Moving a thousand miles away from family meant that we had to get creative, and Christmas Eve could be anything we wanted it to be. It was a heady proposition. What was our hearts' desire?

My pre-Vermont Christmases were special. But seldom were they very snowy. In our old St. Louis lives, Christmas snow was a thing to be wished for and sung about, but not a thing that you actually usually got. Come December up here, the days are mostly all a run of silvery pewter with lazy snowfalls coming in early and often. So some decisions didn't have to be made. It is always a Mountain Christmas around here, and dog walks in the woods are a Christmas Eve staple.

There is usually homemade eggnog in the morning, cappuccino for some, and café au lait for others. There is always a last gasp of tree praise as we ooh and aah over the ornaments we've all collected over the years. They hang next to the ornaments that the kids made in kindergarten and the bright white star that has traveled with this family our whole lives.

There is a lot of repetition in our celebrations. And this, too, is apparently just how we like it. The kids call us in the weeks leading up to the holiday, wanting to know if we've made any of the roszke yet? Are the dogs wearing Christmas collars? Did you guys get the lights up before the snowstorm? How big is the tree?

Here or far away, they are part of the planning. Email may be newfangled, but it connects us in the same old-fashioned and time-honored ways. Texting does, too. I admit it. My kids taught me how. And anyway, the technology doesn't matter. Only the connection does.

We trade notes about menus. (Which roughly means that I see new recipes I want to

convene at the tree at about six and take pictures. Then we each choose one gift from under the tree. Sometimes it is the one you were hoping to find. Lots of shaking and rattling and guessing and suggestions. By six thirty, we are on the road headed to Ludlow, to the Downtown Grocery.

It probably doesn't surprise anyone that I found a tradition for Christmas Eve. We made this one up the first year we moved to Vermont.

We choose a favorite fancy restaurant and take one present each. For a bunch of years, it was the now-defunct Three Clock Inn. Then it was Solo, a local farm-to-table joint that took over Three Clock's space. They make some of the best pork belly I have ever eaten anywhere. Eli loved their flatiron steak so much, he would order two. Every year. And we let him. We may have helped him eat it. Somehow it always all disappeared.

Then, Rogan Lechthaler moved back to the North Country after he fell in love with Abby and sold his Mississippi girl on the wonders of Vermont, and the Downtown Grocery grabbed our hearts. We drink champagne and make toasts to the year we have had and the one that is coming. We give in to the sparkle and glamour that delicious food, candles, silver, linen, flowers, pretty clothes, and little trinkets of love can reliably produce. We open our presents and leave full and happy.

We get home with time for more eggnog, maybe a late-night viewing of *Christmas in Connecticut,* or a fire in front of the tree. John and I move away from the group and have the same old alone time we have always managed, even without Santa and his reindeer to get them all into bed. Everyone drifts off into their own holiday space for a while. Sometimes we read one of the old Christmas books out loud. Benjamin usually has one more thing to wrap. His gifts are always in foil in a goofy, lasting tradition of his very own. When it has been a sunshiny day, we bundle up and sit out on the balcony looking at the Christmas Eve stars.

Christmas is more of a feeling than it is anything else. But it moves so fast. Some years it can feel like it is getting away from you. There is too much. Too much hustle, too much beauty, too

much mess, too much noise, even too much joy. You can't get ahold of it. All you can do is feel . . . as it blows over you. Time won't slow down. But I've learned to expect more out of life than just this jumbled rush of feeling at Christmas. So here's a secret. There is a moment—probably sometime around midnight on Christmas Eve—when time stops. The whole world takes a breath, just at that one moment, and everything feels divine.

Some people find it at church, holding their candle and singing "Silent Night." I bumped into it one year while looking up at the stars with John. Pay attention. It's like with the reindeer. You have to be listening.

The thing is, and this is really the whole point, I guess, whether your tradition is more about Christ's birth or Saint Nick . . . it is Christmas. It is a time marked by stories of generosity and sacrifice. This whole big idea has lasted a long time and it can stand up to a little opposition from the hip curmudgeonly crowd. Lots of us are filled up to the brim with goodwill and hope. We crave a little dazzle. We lift our voices together in joyful song because Christmas reminds us more powerfully than any other holiday about delight. The cookies and the sleigh rides, the meals and the presents are just the devices.

Christmas does not need ordering and improving any more than my snow does. Just mix up a batch of eggnog, squint at some lights, throw in a little Ella, maybe some holly boughs, and you've just about got it. Too many of us try to make Christmas perfect, but the thing is, it comes pretty perfect all by itself.

Christmas Eve Brunch

One of the best ways to have a happy holiday experience is to lay the table. You plan to have fun and then do it. Even when it is just the five of us we start Christmas Eve with a festive brunch. That morning table tells everybody that something special is happening here and we are all about to have some big fun—so get ready! There are recipes here for when it is just your closest family and others for when you are expecting a crowd. They all have two things in common. They taste good and feel special.

Prosciutto Gruyère Fennel Brioche

John and I were in New York City with the kids for Christmas Adventure. We like to look for new spots to eat in whatever neighborhoods we are traveling. One great year when we were all getting haircuts in Hell's Kitchen, we discovered Sullivan Street Bakery. We'd had their bread at restaurants around town, so we were due for a pilgrimage to the source. We walked in the door and were hit smack in the face with the tantalizing smells of bread baking and dough rising. They were serving up a canotto with brioche dough, Gruyère, prosciutto, fennel seed, and mascarpone that morning and we were all eating them like crazy. We bought a box to take back to Vermont. We polished those off in the car on the way home. I had to learn how to make them in self-defense. These are pretty close.

Makes 64 mini rolls

Warm the milk slightly (to no more than 120 degrees). Stir in the yeast and let sit for 5 minutes.

In a large mixing bowl, combine 1½ cups of the flour, sugar, lemon peel, and salt. Stir in the yeast mixture, butter, eggs, the ¼ cup of Gruyère, and the ½ cup of prosciutto. Add another 1 cup of the flour and beat until smooth. Stir in the remaining flour, but do not knead.

Spoon dough into a greased bowl and cover. Let rise in a warm place for about an hour. This will make for a yellow, gooey mess. Yes, it is supposed to look like this.

Gently punch dough down, cover, and refrigerate overnight. (If you're pressed for time, put dough in the freezer uncovered for at least one hour, and then use the harder dough on top for a first batch, putting the rest back in the freezer while each batch bakes.)

INGREDIENTS

½ cup milk

2 packages (¼ ounce each) active dry yeast

3½ cups flour

½ cup sugar

1 teaspoon grated lemon peel

½ teaspoon salt

⅔ cup butter, melted

5 eggs

continued on next page

continued from previous page

¼ cup grated Gruyère, plus at least another ¼ cup for the filling and for sprinkling

½ cup good prosciutto, chopped into small pieces, plus another ½ cup for the filling

Lots of fennel seeds

Mascarpone (Buy a goodly size container. You are going to just use smears here but you will find lots of uses for the leftovers.)

Punch dough down and turn onto a lightly floured surface. Cut a batch-sized swath from the dough and set the rest aside. Divide the dough into 16 equally sized small balls. Cut each of these balls into 4 pieces. Roll these into balls and place on a parchment-lined cookie sheet that has been covered in fennel seeds. You can also dip the bottom of the balls into the fennel before placing them on the pan.

Using your fingers, press a good-sized dab of mascarpone into the dough, making a dent in the ball and a disk on the paper. Cover your dough top with some of the Gruyère. Then add 5 or 6 pieces of prosciutto atop the cheese and inside the dough. Sprinkle a little more fennel on top just for good measure.

Next, gently pull a little of the stretchy dough from one side of the roll to the other. You can do this in a couple of places. It will look messy. Don't worry; it will bake beautifully. You just want a little of the stretchy dough from one side touching the stretchy dough on the other.

Sprinkle grated Gruyère all over the top and inside. If it looks messy and there is some Gruyère on the sides and on the parchment paper you will get those baked cheesy pieces hanging off the edges of your pastry. Don't worry. Everybody loves these!

Bake at 375 degrees for about 12 minutes or until golden brown.

Strata

These came from Benjamin's dad's side of the family at Christmas. Their Christmas Eve brunch, which always included all of us, also always included his grandfather's cheese strata. It was a simple, good mix of bread, cheese, and eggs. Satisfying. There are as many versions of strata as there are cooks. This is an easy and good one.

Butter a 9 x 11-inch baking dish. Remove crust from the bread. Line the bottom of the dish with the bread. Add a layer of cheese, basil, tomatoes, and salt and pepper, and then another layer in that order. Then sprinkle with cheese on top.

Whisk together eggs, milk, melted butter, cayenne, and salt and pepper. Cover tightly with plastic wrap and refrigerate overnight. (If you are in a rush, refrigerate for at least 4 hours.)

Preheat oven to 325 and bake for about 40 minutes, until puffy and golden. Let it rest out of the oven for about 10 minutes prior to serving.

INGREDIENTS

2 to 3 tablepoons butter, melted, plus some for greasing dish

12 slices of white bread

1½ cups grated sharp cheddar

1½ cups grated Gruyère

4 tablespoons chopped fresh basil

2 tomatoes, cut into medium-thick slices

Salt and pepper, to taste

6 eggs (or 8 . . . you decide)

2 cups whole milk

½ teaspoon cayenne pepper

Mock Cheese Soufflé

We had a version of this at our house when I was growing up. It was called the No Fail Soufflé and was the one that filled ramekins with sharp sharp sharp Cheddar when it was Mom's turn to host club. But it wasn't until I saw my great friend Julia Reed whip one of these up right in my own kitchen that I saw the genius. You get the same light, puffy burst of salty cheese flavor in just about half the time. It rises perfectly every single time too. Plus it falls slow. I had stolen it as my own by the very next weekend. What? I'm giving credit here when it really counts.

INGREDIENTS

Butter, for the ramekins and for the bread

8 slices of crustless white bread

1 pound sharp cheddar, grated

4 large eggs

¾ teaspoon salt

2 cups whole milk

2 teaspoons Worcestershire

Dash of cayenne

Butter 8 ramekins. Butter one side of each bread slice and fit a piece of the bread butter-side-up into the bottom of each ramekin. Follow with a layer of cheese, then another piece of the bread, then another layer of cheese.

Make a custard by beating eggs, salt, milk, Worcestershire, and cayenne and pour evenly in each ramekin. Cover tightly with plastic wrap. Refrigerate overnight.

Preheat oven to 350 degrees. Bring ramekins to room temperature and bake until top is brown and soufflé is bubbling, about 35 minutes.

Oysters with Strawberry Mignonette

People will remember this mignonette. It is a standout. The glorious riot of red is where it starts, but the tang of the vinegar next to the sweetness of the berries and the heat of the pepper behind the brininess of the oyster is almost too many good flavors to take in all at once. But you don't have to. Because they merge into a sweet little symphony of taste. It is a perfect bite.

To make the mignonette, mix together peppercorns, vinegar, shallots, salt, sugar, and strawberry salsa.

Shuck the oysters not long before serving. Lay the shells atop a bed of ice. Serve with mignonette sauce on the side.

INGREDIENTS

1 tablespoon coarsely ground peppercorns

¼ cup champagne vinegar

2 tablespoons finely chopped shallots

Good sea salt to taste

1 teaspoon sugar

2 tablespoons strawberry salsa (recipe follows)

Fresh, raw oysters (However many you want. I usually figure 4 to 6 oysters per person depending on what else I'm serving. People always eat way more of these than you think they will.)

Strawberry Salsa

This is part of the mignonette, but I always make a larger batch to serve separately with tortilla chips as a snack. It's very good salsa all by itself, and it tastes good on top of any flaky grilled whitefish too.

INGREDIENTS

- 1 quart strawberries
- 1 cucumber
- 1 jalapeño, finely diced

Salt and pepper to taste

½ to ¾ cup light brown sugar, to taste

- 1 big bunch of finely chopped cilantro

In a food processor, coarsely mix all ingredients. Voilà!

Maple Pepper Bacon

Bacon is why I could never be a successful vegetarian. I love animals. I sometimes wish I didn't eat them. But then . . . bacon. This recipe is practically a love poem.

Serves 4

Preheat oven to 375.

Arrange bacon in a layer, not overlapping, in a baking dish. Bake until fat is rendered, but the bacon is not yet crisp. This takes about 5 to 10 minutes. (I know that's a big range but it depends on the bacon.)

Remove from oven and drain bacon on paper towels. Return bacon to a clean baking dish. Brush the bacon with maple syrup and sprinkle with pepper. Put it back in the oven until it is crisp, about 20 to 25 minutes. Flip it a couple of times while it bakes to ensure syrup soaks into both sides.

INGREDIENTS

16 bacon slices

Maple syrup

Pepper

The Nap Song

Lemme tell ya a story 'bout a No-Nap Jones
He didn't take a nap and he had some weary bones
His friends all said
He forgot to take a snooze
And he fell sound asleep
A-lacin' up his shoes
Hightops, that is,
Red hightops . . .

Chapter Nine

Keeping Christmas

Once the children have grown old enough to sleep in, Christmas changes a bit. Used to be, the rule was that you could not go below the third step from the top of the stairs till everybody else was up. So Hannah and Eli would sit and strain to see what Santa might have left unwrapped under the tree. Lots of years we would hear them running breathlessly back up just as one of us rounded the corner. Good sneaking was all part of the fun.

There were other rules, naturally. Nobody Starts Opening Presents Till Mom and Dad Get Their Coffee was a good one. These days, everyone wants coffee. I carry the nut roll into the library along with the cream cheese, small plates, and kielbasa. It is a slow morning, and fortification will be required.

We take turns handing out the gifts, watching and giving commentary to one another along the way. Our gift giving tends to reflect the same kinds of long-established patterns the rest of the holiday does. John and I always find each other old books by authors we don't yet know. Somebody usually gets me some good stuff for the bath. My perfect Christmas includes bubbles and books by noon.

Santa usually does something silly like get everyone a Nerf gun, which we will all use in the woods on one another by afternoon. For a few years, there was a loud silly electronic thing called Bop It, which was the bassline of a whole bunch of Christmas mornings. There is usually something musical. Eli likes the guitar and Benjamin likes a new harmonica every once in a while.

Hannah likes party clothes that she wouldn't spring for any other time, and a new craft or project to learn. Benjamin usually wants something to do with fishing. Eli likes toys. He always has. So Christmas is a time to figure out what kind of toy might still work for the growing mancub. Poker extravagances are one, and electronic gadgets are another. Since two of the kids have their own homes now, kitchen stuff is always welcome. I have been amassing collections of favorite cookbooks on eBay for all of them, along with one really good pan now and then.

We have our old stockings hung on the mantel, and only Santa puts presents inside them. There is usually some decadent chocolate and something little and silly that only Santa knows your heart desires. This year, Benjamin got a Batman money clip in an ode to childhood love. When Hannah was twelve, her stocking was filled with pots of lipgloss and nail polish in brighter colors than Mom allowed. Santa made the exception.

The point of presents is not how many or how much or even what kind. The point is to demonstrate that you love your people, that you see them, that they are known. So even in lean years, we can make one another happy with homemade recipe files and short stories featuring one another as characters.

Our tags are a favorite part of the whole shebang. We write little hints and funny notes. We draw caricatures and Santa leaves secret messages. Then on Christmas morning, we each read our tags out loud before even the first

weren't, truth be told, managing it very well. Plus, it was Christmas. We might have had a few nerves.

Just to put it all in context, John was grumpy from the surgery. I wanted to throw a perfect, real old-fashioned Christmas in New England for all of us. Perfect, mind you. Benjamin was newly away to college and dying to be home for a family visit in his new home, which he had barely even seen since school started. John's mom was visiting, and she had these perfectly reasonable needs, that somehow her family weren't meeting. Hannah was a teenager who had just moved across the country, leaving all her friends behind. Oh, and Benjamin's dad, and maybe his dad's sister, were flying in later that week.

Only Eli was acting normally at our place.

I was, well, me.

I am, on my best day, excitable. I just am. And it was Christmas. Plus, I was in the middle of changing my whole family's lives with a plan that wasn't just perfectly clear. "Plan" might not be the right word. When you jump from a stable platform onto another stable platform, that's a plan. Point A to Point B. When you do that without looking too closely at what is holding up Point B . . . well, then you don't so much have a plan as you have gravity. And gravity is not actually a good plan. So, though I had been

ready to ju
life thing r
mas. I was j
normal. Fo

Anyway
wine and w
pizza, since
quiet state
was going t
and fed all
grabbed the
glasses. An
been a littl
past couple
nice long w
cold" eveni
trick. It did

First I d
Just one or t

John mi
on a roll. T
indignation

". . . and
versation?
she ask abo
ordering p
didn't you s

It might
was suppos
ing with me

corner is torn. One especially busy year, I got a teenager to help me wrap our presents. They were beautiful. They had little bits of birch and pinecones and were the prettiest presents we had ever had.

But the name cards stunk.

They said things like *For John. Love, Ellen.* Hannah showed her brothers, and all agreed that I should be fired as Christmas Mom that year. I tore them all off and replaced them with their correct personalized versions, every single one.

For Hannahbella don't forget your tiara.

For Benjamin, Pow! Bam! Love, Santa.

That year there was a beach game hidden in one that said, *For Eli Wear Sunscreeen!*

I got to keep my job, but only by the skin of my teeth. They still joke and grumble about The Year Mom Lost Her Mind and Let Someone Else Help with Our Presents. Moving slowly, sipping eggnog, and telling our stories is, after all, the point. We are making up new ones all the time, every single year.

Having celebrated Christmas some fifty-two times now, I fancy myself as something of an expert. An old-fashioned Christmas may be a bit about magic, but it can also be at least a little bit about old-fashioned strife and new resentments. We can get so caught up in all our hopes and expectations that a burned din-

ner can seem like a calamity, not just an extra crispy goose.

Christmas is a time for magic and generosity and love and all that other good and worthwhile stuff. But let's face it, it can also be a time for getting really good and mad. Christmas is big and roomy. It can hold it all. There is an awful lot of proximity and sometimes there are a few little vexing disappointments bumped right up next to the good stuff. The men I am related to can wrestle and poke one another and work it out on the floor. But it's the women who always make the biggest messes. We use fake smiley poison word darts that can kill at ten paces, easy. Men are much more obliging than we are. With us, it's all about what you said, what you didn't say, and what I just know you are thinking and you might as well go ahead and say 'cause I am going to be mad anyway.

Look, Christmas is that time of year when all the folks you love come together—sometimes in your house—and spread love with equal parts anxiety. It happens. I love Christmas. But it's also true that it can make me a little crazy.

The first year we were living in Vermont was one of . . . those. We didn't have jobs or any foreseeable way of making a living. I'd sold my business and bought a house. But hadn't yet figured how we were going to make a living. We were also celebrating the holidays in a beautiful place, where we knew practically no one. To add to the fun, John had just had some sort of oral surgery and was taking painkillers.

And we figured that since we were in this new home, we should invite John's mom to come to Vermont for Christmas. It would be fun to have her, of course, and she'd be able to enjoy this new experience with us. (We—I—also invited my ex-husband and his sister—but more on that later.)

John's mom, Dorothy, has always been the kind of woman who bakes Christmas cookies every year by the caseload. Every year, she mails us all big, happy boxes of this sugary goodness. During John's childhood she spent most Decembers in her kitchen, singing along to "Winter Wonderland" as she stirred. It was a happy kitchen because she was in it. John loves Christmas, and Dorothy was the first reason why.

She loved John's father, too. They had a good marriage. John remembers how on Friday nights, he and his four older brothers would have a fun kid supper of homemade pizza or hot dogs with green eggs (a kid-friendly way to sneak in a little spinach). His parents would sit down later at the table with the radio playing, and they would have the shrimp his dad had driven to St. Louis for on his way home from work. Once in a while, Dorothy would cut John off a little taste of what they were eat-

ing before
could have
has served

Doroth
has long ha
know, ther
feel entitle
five. Her lis
planning o
able to cur
indulgentl
wolf whist
made up n
has a certa
includes a
on-time dir

That's r
place, we t
have lots c
fire tending
and their f
the lead-up
which is, co
certain, but
ing of the d
dogs when
also be less
decades of l

Still, we
ing on this

Patsy) once told me that it is in all ways better to want what you get. I love that because she's right.

Sometime later, probably when you are in your forties if you have done it right, you will figure out that the Rolling Stones were also right, and while you can't always get what you want, what you have is what you would have wanted all along if only you had known how good it was going to be.

After all the presents, we each amble off again for a while. I usually aim for a lazy bubble bath and some reading. Then, of course, there's a little more cooking. Or anyway, the laying out of the already cooked happens. Sometimes we get dressed and sometimes we don't. People drop by, the kinds of people who have already seen us in our jammies. There are usually the kids' friends home from college. Sometimes our Jewish friends stop in, maybe feeling a little left out. These are the faces of our regular lives, our year.

There is always a buffet on the counter and a game of something going in the library. We have

a highly competitive backgammon tournament all day, with some serious high-stakes betting. Girlfriends and boyfriends come round on their nicest behavior and we look them over to check for a possible fit. (There are a couple of newbies on the scene right now who seem to have possibilities. I have my fingers crossed.)

Christmas is slower with nearly grown kids who don't have their own families yet. The hustle and bustle of the early, sleepless years are behind John and me. It's still ahead for the kids. But we can rest on our haunches a bit and trust in our routines.

At some point everyone heads outside and we walk the dogs, throw a ball around, hop on the sleds, or shoot one another with Nerf darts for a while before wandering back in and eating just a little more. 'Cause, after all, we are all gonna be dead a long time.

By evening, we have sung our last tribute to chestnuts roasting. It is time to bring out the New Orleans jazz or some rowdy blues. The music changes over, and just like that another Christmas has been kept.

Christmas All Day Long

Everyone has traditional foods that are their family's favorites. Over here it's Runny Eggs Bennie with prosciutto and arugula on top of homemade biscuits. That meal makes us all feel instantly festive and party-ready. And turkey always makes the house smell divine. I only cook in the late morning . . . everything else sort of cooks itself or gets laid out from an earlier kitchen session. That way there is plenty of time in front of the fire with my new Christmas book and a dog keeping my feet warm. Time too for a snowy walk in the woods before evening comes and folks are ready to eat again. Christmas is about what we love the most. Or it oughta be anyway. And this is some of what I love best of all.

Café au Lait

It's all about the foam.

Makes 1 serving

INGREDIENTS

8   ounces coffee

¼   cup milk

Dash of nutmeg, cinnamon,
   or cocoa powder

Prepare coffee any ol' way you like. Use your milk frother to foam milk (1 percent milk makes the best foam) and pour over coffee. Sprinkle your favorite spice on top and serve hot.

Cheddar Soufflé

When I was a kid, Sunday dinner was the noontime meal served right after church. Come Advent, we always had the minister and his family over at least once. My mom used to make these along with roast beef for one of the December Sunday dinners. I loved how they tasted and also how tall they were. This was food that had been gussied up for the Christmas company. Mom's trick was to fold in the beaten egg whites right away, before they had a chance to deflate. She also kept a copper bowl just for whisking her egg whites. I can still see that little bowl. I wonder what happened to it.

INGREDIENTS

- 2½ tablespoons butter, and some for the dish
- 2 tablespoons grated Parmesan
- 1 cup milk
- 3 tablespoons flour
- Dash of paprika
- Dash of salt
- Dash of nutmeg
- 4 large egg yolks
- 5 big fat egg whites
- 1 cup grated sharp Cheddar (Gruyère is a fine alternative)

Preheat oven to 400 degrees.

Butter a 1½-quart soufflé dish. Coat the bottom with parmesan and tilt the dish so it comes up the sides. Heat the milk in medium saucepan until it is steaming, not boiling. Then turn down the heat.

Meanwhile, melt the butter in heavy saucepan over medium heat. Add flour and whisk hard, making a roux. Do not allow it to brown. Remove from heat and let it cool for a minute. Then add the warm milk and whisk until smooth. Put back on heat and keep whisking until very thick. Then remove from heat and add paprika, salt, and nutmeg. Add egg yolks, one at a time, whisking after each. Then move to bowl and let mixture cool to room temperature.

Beat egg whites until they're stiff. Fold about a third of the egg whites into the yolk mixture. Then add another third. Then add Cheddar and then add last third of egg whites. Transfer to prepared dish.

Place in oven and turn temperature down to 375. Leave the oven door open for a few seconds to lower the temp. Bake until golden brown and puffy. *Do not stomp around or open the oven door until finished cooking. Serve immediately or else it will fall.*

Tagliatelle

You'll use this in the next recipe.

INGREDIENTS

2   cups flour

1   teaspoon salt

5 or 6 egg yolks

1½ teaspoons olive oil

On a clean, dry work surface, form the flour into a mound, 8 to 10 inches in diameter at the base. Add salt.

Create a well or open space for wet ingredients. Gently pour the yolks and olive oil into the flour well, using a fork to gently beat the eggs without touching the flour walls. After the eggs are beaten, slowly incorporate the flour.

Once the dough is thick, slide a wooden spatula or paddle under the dough and flip it. Knead the dough for 10 to 15 minutes with the heels of your hands. Pasta is easy to underknead but impossible to overknead. When the dough is ready, it will stop changing appearance and texture.

Roll dough into a ball and tightly wrap with plastic. Let the wrapped dough rest for at least 30 minutes at room temperature. If not using immediately, refrigerate and use within 24 hours.

Cut off a section of the dough (enough to make about a pound of pasta; rewrap the rest) and roll out with rolling pin. Gently feed into pasta machine and hang noodles to dry. Cut into desired length.

Sage Pancetta Tagliatelle

Keith McNally is my favorite chef. He makes the foods I crave . . . especially for people who battle low cholesterol. I ate something like this at his Minetta Tavern and it was the perfect tangle of salt and cream. John improved it by cutting the sage into long beautiful curling ribbons. Saucing eggy pasta with an egg is almost too much of a good thing. So this is actually best as a small plate.

You will need a pasta maker for the tagliatelle. Of course, you could use a good dried pasta instead. But making your own is fast and easy and I promise you will taste more delicious than all the good food words could possibly convey.

Makes 4 servings

INGREDIENTS

6 ounces pancetta, cut into 1-inch pieces

2 fat bunches of sage

2 to 3 cloves garlic, minced

½ cup mascarpone

Salt for pasta water

1 pound tagliatelle (see page 232)

Salt and freshly ground pepper, to taste

4 large eggs

Parmigiano-Reggiano, grated, for sprinkling

Sauté the pancetta till slightly crisp. Roll sage into long ribbons, chop, and add to the pancetta; sauté for about a minute. Add the garlic and sauté for about thirty or forty seconds only, so it does not burn. Mix in the mascarpone.

Bring pot of water to boil (add a handful of salt to remove starchiness) and cook 1 pound of pasta till al dente (it should feel nutty in your mouth). Drain.

Toss pasta with pancetta and sage mixture and season with salt and freshly ground pepper. Serve with lightly fried egg and a sprinkling of Parmigiano-Reggiano on top to sauce.

Grandma Rimarchik's Slovak Day Bread

One December when Hannah was in sixth grade, she had to deliver a demonstration speech. She decided she would do hers on Grandma's bread. We just needed a recipe. When the day came she had four big bowls going and adorable little teams of eleven-year-olds kneading dough. All four loaves turned out perfectly. She even braided one. I had married her dad for this dough and now, here we all were, a decade and a half and three kids later. It was one of the sweetest moments of my life. When I make that bread now I still use the recipe written in Hannah's eleven-year-old hand the day I taught her to make the dough. She measured each ingredient as I poured it so she would have a recipe. We did this book the same way, 'cause I still don't know how much of anything I use. Talk about a Christmas legacy.

INGREDIENTS

- ¼ cup whole milk, warmed, plus ¾ cup cold
- 1 (½ ounce) packet yeast
- ½ teaspoon sugar, plus ½ cup
- 2 eggs
- 3½ cups flour
- ½ teaspoon salt
- ½ teaspoon baking soda
- ½ cup butter

Add the ¼ cup of warmed milk to yeast with a pinch of sugar and set aside to rise. In a separate bowl, beat eggs and add ½ cup sugar. Blend well. Sift flour, salt, and baking soda and slowly add to the eggs. Add butter and the ¾ cup of milk. Mix and add yeast mixture, forming the dough.

If the dough is too wet, add flour. Put dough on a clean, floured surface and knead for 5 to 10 minutes, getting all the air bubbles out. Roll it into a ball and place into a greased bowl. Flip it, so both sides are greased. Cover and let rest in a draft-free area until the dough has doubled in size.

Preheat oven to 325.

When the dough has doubled, punch it down and place in a
greased bread pan and bake 25 to 35 minutes until golden brown.
Remove from pan and let cool.

Baked Eggs

When you raise chickens, inevitably there comes a time every summer when all you do is make up new egg recipes. When the days are long, the chickens lay like crazy, and even after giving fresh eggs to all your friends and neighbors, it is about all you can do just to keep up. These egg-rich recipes get invented and perfected during that time and then are trotted out during the holidays when company comes and the eggs are not so plentiful on the ground. No matter. Sure these are better with fresh eggs (pretty much everything is) but they are just fine made from the store-bought variety as well.

Serves 6

INGREDIENTS

Butter for the ramekins, and more for the soldiers

About ¼ cup heavy cream

Salt and pepper

Dried tarragon

6 eggs

Heat oven to 375 degrees.

Butter 6 ramekins. Add a dot of cream, salt and pepper, and dried tarragon to the bottom of each ramekin. Crack an egg into each one. Add more salt, pepper, and tarragon. Top eggs with 1 tablespoon of cream each.

Fill a baking dish halfway with water. Put ramekins in dish. Bake for 10 to 15 minutes until whites are set but yolks are still soft. (If you want, you can sauté mushrooms, onions, shallots, or bacon, and add. You can top with pretty much anything you want.)

Serve with soldiers (buttered toast cut into thin strips that you can dip in the eggs).

Ham Glaze

Really, nowadays, there is practically no reason to cook a ham. There is nothing wrong with a good, ready-to-eat cooked ham, bone-in, uncut. And just let me tell you this particular old-fashioned ham glaze will make anything taste delicious. Just add it to your cooked ham when you are warming it up.

You can make some ham biscuits with a little homemade pimento cheese or Gruyère and your guests will imagine you slaved all night.

INGREDIENTS

- 2 tablespoons cornstarch
- 1 cup chicken stock
- 3 tablespoons butter
- 3 shallots, minced
- Pinch of allspice
- 4 cups dark stout
- 1 cup brown sugar
- 1 cup dried cherries
- ½ tablespoon balsamic vinegar
- Salt and pepper to taste

Whisk cornstarch into chicken stock in a saucepan over medium-low heat.

In a separate saucepan, melt butter and throw in shallots. Cook shallots for a few minutes, then add a pinch of allspice and cook about thirty seconds more. Add the stout, brown sugar, and dried cherries. Simmer sauce till it thickens, about 15 minutes. Then whisk the cornstarch mixture again and add it gradually to the stout mixture. Cook for about 10 minutes over low heat, stirring often.

Remove from heat once thick and dark and smoky-looking, and add balsamic vinegar and salt and pepper. Puree. It should have a fruity blackish bitter-at-the-end flavor.

Kugel

Kugel works no matter what you are celebrating. This is about as close as I can get to my gram's kugel. I have added a grated apple some years but, while tasty, I don't actually think hers had any. She cooked with her hands and her heart and didn't write many of the old recipes down. Me neither. But this is close. . . .

Preheat the oven to 375 degrees.

Boil the noodles in salted water for about 4 minutes. Strain noodles from water. In a large mixing bowl, combine noodles with all other ingredients and pour into a greased baking dish.

Bake until custard is just set and the top is golden brown, about 30 to 45 minutes.

INGREDIENTS

½ pound wide egg noodles

½ stick melted butter

1 pound cottage cheese

2 cups full-fat sour cream

½ cup sugar

6 fat eggs

A little cinnamon

A tiny dash of nutmeg

½ cup raisins

Snow Leopard

During his homeschooling years, Eli did a research project on cats. As part of the project, he was to uncover the best possible cat breed for an eight-year-old boy. He decided Bengals were just made for eight-year-old boys. It turns out that they are pretty good for nineteen-year-old boys and their middle-aged parents, too.

Sadiecat is in all ways a family cat. She meows hello to each one of us every morning and is as cuddly with all of us as she is with any one of us. She loves Olive, Benjamin's dog, with a passion.

They are unlike any mixed-species relationship I have ever known. They run and play, lick and cuddle, and are as totally bonded as any people I know.

Snow Leopard is an homage to Sadie. Of course, since it is enormous and delicate it belongs to Eli, but like her namesake she somehow belongs to us all. Despite living on the heaviest branches at the bottom of the tree, she doesn't even have a crack.

Like the rest of us, she is sturdier than she looks.

Chapter Ten

The Day After

Where did Christmas go? It happened so fast. All that's left are bits of silvery glitter in the dogs' fur. Looks like fairies dropped by and something wonderful happened. Leave it. Let it sparkle a while.

'Cause here's another great thing about Christmas.

The day after.

Some people rush off to go shopping and hit all the sales. They love to get stores of wrapping paper and bargains for the next year. I am not one of those people. I don't even want to get dressed the day after. I think it can be difficult to find and hold onto the meaning in our celebrations in the midst of the consumer culture. Don't get me wrong, I like to shop as much as the next person. And I'm always happy to find gifts that make my people happy. But a visiting Martian might be justified in thinking that Christmas is about new smartphones and iPods, Xboxes and malls. Lots of people get out of bed at 4:00 AM on Black Friday to go to Best Buy to get a new TV at a good price. It is a huge part of their own Christmas Adventure. Why not? If your idea of big fun is to get together with your people and shop for bargains, then do that. Go early, make lists, eat cheesecake. Have a ball.

One of the great things about being a grown-up at Christmas is that we get to pick the celebrations we want to have. I know some women who plan their after-Christmas shopping all year. These women strategize. They get babysitters, scope out bargains, plot their store routes, and stuff their pockets with measuring tapes, magnifying glasses, water bottles, and snacks. Then they hit the sales. They are generals planning their attack. These folks have great stories of tips and wins. Of the year they got the (insert product name here) when practically no one else did.

The point of this whole exercise we call Christmas is to figure out what feels fun and sweet to you and do more of that and less of anything that feels like a burden.

Delight. You are going for delight.

When the kids are little, the day after Christmas is a school holiday. There is no pressure to see family, or even get dressed. Parents can play with the new toys, too, and eat peanut butter sandwiches all day if they want. There are no parties or concerts or shopping to do. There are no dinners to cook and plenty of leftovers still to eat. You can even take a nap. The post-Christmas nap is almost a requirement. The day after Christmas is practically a holiday all by itself. It is a day of freedom from expectation and it comes with new stuff to play with. How great is that?

One year, when work was piling up along with a few worries and a ton of bills in the months leading up to Christmas, I wrote to all of the kids and asked them which of our traditions mattered the most. I intended to make a few cuts. If we could only do one thing from our list, what would you want it to be? Then tell me what two and three would be too.

It turned out that Christmas Adventure mattered, and so did Christmas Eve supper out. But the holiday party, not so much. The tree mattered the most, so the new ornaments had to stay. Cookies were requirements for most of us, but actually only two or three kinds as opposed to the dozens of varieties I had always thought we needed. The biggest surprise was the day after Christmas. Everyone wanted a quiet jammie day of movies and Chinese food.

Most years we try to find ourselves one new family gift. It can be a movie or a game but it has to be something we can all do together. One year the gift was a collection of newly released *Seinfeld* episodes. The day after Christmas was a *Seinfeld* marathon. The next year it was *Curb Your Enthusiasm*. Those were hysterically fun days spent by the fire. We had all gotten a giant cold that we kept passing back and forth and so we ate soup beside the fire and giggled our way back to well.

When the snow is still falling hard and you don't have anywhere to be, it feels like permission from "the authorities" to snuggle in. Use your imagination. It doesn't have to twenty-eight-below in snowy New England. It can be whatever you want it to be.

The library is my second home. We are both a book and game family. So if it's winter and we're not in the kitchen, then there is a fire in the library and you can find us in there with the dogs. We play chess and backgammon and Taboo and Scrabble. John is a great pinochle partner, and can I just say pinochle is a pretty sexy way to spend an evening? You have to know what your partner is thinking, and when he winks at you it is your own special secret.

One of our friends invited us over on Boxing Day this year, but we turned them down. We love those people and have fun with them. I think it may have hurt their feelings when I said we wanted to just snuggle in with each other. My friend wondered wasn't that what we'd been doing? She was right. It was. She might have used the word "clannish." I bet she didn't say it, but I heard it all the same.

The truth of the matter is not that we want to get away from our friends, but rather go toward time with just each other. Sacred family time. Getting dressed and going out is hard when all I really want to do is snuggle up in John's arms by the fire beside the tree with our kids and animals all around. It is selfish. And it is true. I love being with these people.

It is what it is.

The day after is as good a time as any to count up blessings instead of sheep. Have everyone in your family make up a Desire List, a list of long-held secret things you want to do but never really talk about. Like, I kind of want a pig. I really think I need one. Not everyone in the family agrees. But each of you can make a list. Then do one thing on everyone's list. It will be lots of fun and you will always remember the day you took the bath in heavy cream.

The Next Day

Avoid the letdown and plan ahead. Doughnuts are fun crowd-pleasers and they make it seem like it is still Christmas. Plus they are a great group activity. Even the youngest kids can help by rolling them in sugar or dipping them in the glaze. I also like to switch it up. So maybe ceviche or a big bowl of ramen for supper. These are not Christmas foods but they are reminders that Christmas is really just a good feeling and there can be lots of those in store all year long. So here we go. . . .

Creamy Tarragon Eggs

We had a little herb garden in the windowsill. The thyme was finicky. So was the rosemary. But the tarragon grew like crazy. So we wound up with a few pots of that. The kids wanted it in their eggs every morning. Swirled into the yolks from our own hens, these are creamy rich comfort on a plate. You'll smell them first. The steam brings out the sweet tang and you won't be able to get enough.

Makes 2 servings

INGREDIENTS

6   eggs
¼   cup heavy cream
Salt and pepper
1   handful of fresh tarragon
1   knob of butter

Beat eggs just until yolks and whites are combined. Add heavy cream. Season with salt and pepper and tarragon.

Heat pan on medium. Add a knob of butter, and after it melts, turn heat to low. Add eggs and cook over low heat, stirring occasionally. After 10 minutes, eggs will begin to form curds. Keep stirring to break up the curds for about 30 minutes.

This is the longest way to make scrambled eggs, but it is also the best way. They will feel like velvet in your mouth. James Beard told me so and I believed him.

Sugar-Glazed Doughnuts

Homemade doughnuts are a production. But they are perfect for the day after when you are coming down from all the excitement. This can be a fun morning activity when you are decorating the tree or wrapping presents too. Bring the kids in and give them scissors and tape and paper while you keep the doughnuts coming. The only downside is that they will remember and ask you to do it again. Year after year.

Makes a baker's dozen, about 13

INGREDIENTS

- ½ package yeast
- ¼ cup lukewarm water (100 degrees)
- ¾ cup of warm milk (100 degrees)
- 1 egg
- 2 tablespoons sugar
- ¼ stick of butter (softened to room temperature) or shortening
- 2 cups flour, and a bit more for rolling
- Vegetable oil for frying

In a large mixing bowl, dissolve yeast in water, then add milk, egg, sugar, butter, and flour. Mix well for a few minutes (electric mixer for 2, or 5 minutes by hand). Cover dough for at least an hour, or overnight for breakfast doughnuts.

On a lightly floured surface, roll out doughnut dough with a rolling pin about ½-inch thick. Cut doughnuts with a cutter (you can use a coffee cup), then a smaller cutter (bottle top) for the centers. You can set aside the doughnut holes with the doughnuts or re-roll them for another doughnut or two. Let cut doughnuts set another half an hour to rise one last time before frying.

In a wide skillet or pot with vegetable oil ½ inch deep (the doughnuts will float), fry doughnuts for 2 or 3 minutes, turning once, until golden brown.

While doughnuts are still warm, coat with sugar glaze.

Sugar Glaze

Melt butter and add to powdered sugar, vanilla, and water. Mix well for a couple of minutes. Pour into shallow dish for dipping/coating warm doughnuts.

INGREDIENTS

¼ stick butter

1 cup powdered sugar

½ teaspoon vanilla

2 tablespoons water (for clear glaze) or milk (for white glaze)

Bay Scallop Ceviche

This stuff is habit-forming. And it is light enough that you will feel virtuous eating it too. It is the perfect antidote to December. You are coming back after a long bout of rich and decadent and these little bits of seashine will remind you of summer and all that's coming next.

INGREDIENTS

⅓ cup lime juice

⅓ cup grapefruit juice

1 cup orange juice

1 cup shallots, finely diced

2 red or green chilies, seeded and minced

1 grapefruit, peeled and sectioned

Sea salt

3 tablespoons coconut flakes, optional (I had these left over from Christmas baking one year and decided to throw them in. I was tickled with the result.)

2 dozen scallops, shucked

¾ cup fresh cilantro, for garnishing

In a bowl, combine lime, grapefruit, and orange juice and mix in shallots, chilies, grapefruit, salt, and coconut flakes, if using. Add raw scallops and marinate, in refrigerator, for a couple of hours.

Spoon ceviche into small glasses and serve cold. Garnish with cilantro.

Lemon Rice Soup

I was a little girl home from school on Christmas vacation, and this was the first soup I ever made. I still crave it right after Christmas, when some years the sun seems to go on vacation. Yellow sunshine in a bowl. Comforting and fresh. This soup will brighten any dreary winter day.

In a 2-quart saucepan, bring broth to a boil. Reduce heat, add rice, cover, and simmer until rice is tender, about 20 minutes.

In a small bowl, beat eggs and lemon juice. Add 1 cup of the hot soup, a little bit at a time, into the egg mixture, stirring constantly.

Stir egg mixture into soup in saucepan and heat (don't let it come to a boil). Season with salt and pepper. Serve immediately.

INGREDIENTS

6 cups chicken broth

⅓ cup uncooked regular rice

4 egg yolks

3 tablespoons lemon juice

Dash of sea salt

Dash of freshly ground pepper

Grilled Onion Pistachio and Lemon Winter Greens

John and I had a version of this at John Harris's popular Lilette in New Orleans. He uses escarole and celery leaf and sunchokes. That pistachio pesto was delicious and I knew immediately how I would make it back home. Mine is a more accessible version you can make any night of the week with whatever greens you have on hand. I make the onions ahead and then just warm them up right before I serve the salad. Salads hardly ever grab people's attention. This one is the exception.

INGREDIENTS

- 3 romaine hearts
- 12 ounces shelled pistachios
- 4 Vidalia onions
- Olive oil
- 3 lemons
- ¼ cup sugar
- Salt and pepper to taste

Chop romaine into bite-sized pieces. Roll shelled pistachios or pulse in food processor.

Slice and sauté onions until clear with brown edges.

Mix pistachios with greens. Drizzle olive oil on greens. Juice 3 lemons and add to salad. Sprinkle a generous handful of sugar on top.

Toss and serve immediately with hot onions. Finish with salt and pepper.

Shining in the East

The first time we broke it, back in our little town of Edwardsville, Illinois, our friend Rick fixed it. We are not a handy people. Years later, it was another Rick, in Vermont, who managed to keep it working for one more year. Then it was Kyle's turn. He came and glued it back together the last time.

How come it doesn't have a little door in back that you can open to change the light? It used to. It doesn't anymore. Now you have to break in to change the light. Commit a little armed robbery. But this glowing three-dimensional white star has traveled with us all these years. It is the first thing we put on the tree when we decorate and the last thing to come off.

When I go outside with the dogs at night in December I always walk up to the top of the hill and look down at our house. It looks so cozy in there with the lights on the tree and that white star shining on top. It feels a little bit like looking in the windows of a doll's house. From the top of the hill, you can't feel the drafty old doorways. All the noise is muted, too. I imagine the people who live there as little characters in a play. I figure they feel snug and probably have a fire going and are reading a good book.

I always think those people must be so happy. And you know what? Most of the time they really are.

Chapter Eleven

Till Next Year

I am not a good mover. In fact, it might be fairer to say I am a terrible mover. About two weeks before the big day, my job is to start crying. John packs boxes, tapes, labels, and stacks, and I cry. At first, I just sort of sniffle over a piece of art I see him wrapping, remembering the day we bought it together, and how happy we were when we first hung it in what was then our new home together. It is just a little teary and nostalgic and I don't yet look like a complete mental patient. That part comes later. By the time the moving truck shows up, I am sobbing over the day one of the kids broke that window over there, remember? This is not something I am particularly proud of but neither is it something I can help.

Putting away Christmas is similar. At least it used to be. I got mopey on New Year's Day when the tree came down. I was okay with wrapping up all the glass beads. They are beautiful and I love them on the tree, but they don't each have their own special story. But the ornaments? They would get me every single time. I'd worry we'd break one of the really important ones. We have. Sometimes it can be replaced on eBay. God bless eBay. But sometimes it can't.

I'd worry that I won't live to see another Christmas. I always have so far, but there's no guarantee, right? I'd worry that this will be the last time we are all together at the holidays. Up to this point, none of the kids has shown any inclination for moving a continent away or anything, but just the sight of all those bins and tissue paper can put me in a mournful mood. I don't know how else to explain it. I am bad at transitions, I guess. I don't like to say goodbye at the airport. And I really do not like putting away Christmas. I don't want it to end. Some years, like the ones where the flu has overtaken our holiday or we all have really bad colds, I have succumbed to my little breakdowns and John has done all the heavy lifting by himself. Truthfully, though, those have not been the only times I have failed at Christmas Put Away.

There were times I imagined getting new, cool bins and wrapping each ornament in a labeled box so we could find these precious things on a moment's notice. I have fantasized that if I ever won the lottery, I would hire one of those closet experts to come in and organize my Christmas. But so far, it is still a fantasy.

Then, some years back, I decided that I was sick of my own self. Sick of the whiny lead-up to the Big Put Away. Sick of the mopey feelings and sick of John doing all the heavy lifting. I was determined to pitch in and follow the old axiom that many hands make light work. John rushed through taking all the ornaments off the tree just like usual, and piled them in big bunches on the couch while they waited in turn for their wrapping and tucking in for another year. Used to be that just the sight of all of our most precious bits piled together on the couch would send me into a tizzy. But not that year. That year I sat and wrapped and tucked and boxed and sorted just like a sane person would. I figured if I acted like a happy, regular person I might feel like one. Pretty much that's how it worked out.

John got the beads off and I made quick work of wrapping those. Then he took the lights off and made neat piles with them. I kept wrapping and tucking in as he and Eli dragged the tree out to the woods. He came back and we finished together with nary a tear, and then I went straight to the kitchen, turned Van up loud, and made us all a happy supper.

I still can't say why that year was different. Or the ones that have come after. Because I have kept up my sane routine in the ensuing couple of years since. The Big Put Away has gone faster and smoother, and I don't think I have shed a single tear. I still think it all looks mournful. And I can even imagine falling apart. But I don't. I am in my fifties now, and I don't have the same sort of appetite for drama that I did in my twenties. It bores me.

Oh, I am still a classic overreactor. I come from a long line of them, and it surely isn't going to get fixed in this one generation. I have a wide emotional range. But I have never liked feeling sad for long. I don't even enjoy crying so much anymore. Your nose gets stuffed up. Your face gets red and puffy, and it almost never does any good.

Somewhere along the way I finally figured out that I could choose to behave a little better, and by golly that made me feel better too. Now I battle the "saying goodbye" experience with loud, zippy New Orleans jazz. A good Marcia Ball album can get you mostly through the ornaments, which are the hardest part. It helps to have a cheery plan for supper that requires doing. Most of all, I plan for the post-holidays winter decor now.

It is too sad for words to take all of Christmas down and not have something around to replace it. So now I collect fresh birch logs and branches and decorate them with mercury glass and candles. While the tree gets carried to the woods, I cut evergreen branches and fill the vases. If I have planned really well, there are pots of narcissus that I've been forcing upstairs, which can come down. And if I have forgotten to plan, then I go to the florist and get white roses, which look gorgeous cut short and tucked in with evergreen and holly.

It helps to invite someone over for supper that night. Our dear pal David Silver is always a good choice at our house. One, the guy shows up. And two, he comes funny. As an added bonus, he will almost always play backgammon.

Another neat thing is that, in the corner where our Christmas tree lives throughout December, an old eighteenth-century wine-tasting table stands the rest of the year. It has a lamp and a chess set on top, and getting that back into place feels good. I love when I can get someone to give me a game, and even better

if I win said game 'cause my opposition knows I am a little sad. The best opponents play with one hand tied behind their back. (Eli.)

Of course, I could go up to the attic and look at the ornaments and feel a little Christmas love any time I wanted. Minnie Mouse is tucked softly in her old wooden box and so is St. Louie Nick.

But I don't. Because part of the secret of keeping Christmas is that Christmas has a timetable. It's a little like the Disney movies were when we were kids. Remember how thrilling it was when *Lady and the Tramp* was rereleased? It was a thrill because it hardly ever happened. Kind of like *The Wizard of Oz* being shown on TV only at Easter. Christmas only comes once a year. We all get our measure of Christmas. I have probably already had more Christmases in my past than I will get in the future. Unless I live to be 105, which doesn't seem exactly likely. But that rarity is what makes Christmas special. We have to put it away to keep it. I get that now.

I have had fifty-two Christmases so far. Most of them have been pretty good. Not all. There have been years when a loss or a worry has overshadowed the big event. But mostly they have been a mix of the sweet and the fun, the irritating and the overwhelming. Just like the rest of my life.

I imagine most of us grown-ups just about get the Christmases we deserve. If we do nice things for people, our lives are generally full up with people who do nice things for us. And in my experience, those people show up at Christmas. They call from far away and send little notes of encouragement. They invite you over for dinner, and they help out when, for example, one of your ratty teenage kids has just done something awful that has set the whole town talking.

Fifty-two. If everything goes according to plan I'll probably get another thirty or so good ones. I think it's a good idea to ask, "How many more Christmases? How will they be spent?"

I guess I'll want to spend mine pretty much the way I always have. I'll want to cook and wrap presents and sit by the fire with the people and animals I love who love me right back.

They make up my tribe. We can eat good stuff together and tell each other our stories. I want to make deviled eggs. I want to squint my eyes at the tree and look for light formations in the branches.

There's a song from *The Sound of Music* that you hear a lot at Christmas. "My Favorite Things." Me? I love the sound of birch crackling in the fire. I love the drawings Eli makes on his Christmas cards. I love Grandma Rimarchik's rolling pin and the way Oscar keeps my feet warm down at his end of the bed. I love when John winks at me and I love when we are all together. I love making dough beside Hannah and I love Benjamin's foil-wrapped presents. I love us at Christmas. Maybe that's the truest thing.

Happy Christmas, Uncle Felix. Happy, happy Christmas.

The Pocket Watch

When John was a little boy, he played with an old golden pocket watch. He was a banker, a writer, and, best of all, a railroad conductor when he wore it. Now, every year, that sweet reminder of his childhood drapes across a couple of branches of our Christmas tree, up high near Minnie.

John was the last of five boys. It was a small house filled to overflowing. He is a quiet introvert by nature and I like to think the cacophony of all those boys got him ready for me. But he loved to play alone when he could. His imagination and gentle, thoughtful brain led the way. That pocket watch marked the time it took for him to grow up. Then he carried it to his first apartment, and to every place we have lived together since. I love this little pocket watch. It is a sweet piece of the history that made the man.

When we have some horrible problem and I am outta my mind—maybe overreacting just a little bit . . . okay, maybe more than just a little bit—he is always the one to predict the future. He will remind me that in a year, maybe two, this will have been a blip. The guy gets time. He will imagine a happier future. Maybe next weekend. Maybe even this afternoon. The watch hangs on our tree like a promise. We have had a time, it seems to say, and here, you still have some Christmas left. How lucky is that?

Winter Adventures in Vermont

Sleigh Rides!

Karl Pfister of **Pfister Farm Sleigh Rides** (www.karlpfistersleigh.com; 802-824-4663; 132 Landgrove Rd., Landgrove, VT 05148) is that Vermonter who knows his stars. He took our family out one Christmas Eve, and John saw Taurus for the first time. It was a gift as memorable as anything under the tree that year. We also peeked at Andromeda. The light we were seeing had traveled millions of years to get to us. What a gentle lesson in perspective. Karl's horses are loved and gorgeous. I promise you that a sleigh ride from his Londonderry barn will delight your whole family. It did ours.

Kedron Valley Stables (www.kedron.com; 802-457-1480; 4342 South Rd., South Woodstock, VT 05071) is another option if you are visiting Woodstock, Vermont. Private carriage rides and sleigh rides through colonial Woodstock will give you the quintessential experience of an old-fashioned New England village.

Country Stores

While you're in Woodstock, be sure to stop in at **Gillingham's** (www.gillinghams.com; 802-457-2100 or 800-344-6668; 16 Elm St., Woodstock, VT 05091). Gillingham's is an old country store established in 1886. You can get a bottle of wine for your picnic here, or old-fashioned puzzles and games for a snowy day at your inn. New

England specialty foods, maple candy, and local boutique cheese are right at home next to muck boots and thick hand-knitted mittens. Get your sled here and keep it in the back of the car alongside a thermos filled with hot cocoa. Vermont is dotted with hillsides just perfect for a little spontaneous side-of-the-road sledding. We all do it, all winter long. You will look just like a local when you hop out of your car and take a quick ride down into someone's pasture. The farmer may come out and invite you in for coffee. Despite the New England reserve you may have heard so much about, Vermonters love Christmastime and we love winter. So we are especially happy when the tourists seem to love it as much as we do.

It is hard to overstate how much I love a trip to Gillingham's. It has a smell that is as old and sweet as anything I have ever smelled anywhere. As a tourist, I always stopped in for winter games and good soap. As a local, I still do.

And of course there is nothin' better than *The Vermont Country Store* (www.vermontcountrystore.com; 802-824-3184; 657 Main St., Weston, VT 05161), the Orton Family Business since 1946. We always take our out-of-town guests here. Park around back, but make sure you use the front door. It is like taking a step back in time. The staff is always friendly and the store feels like every Vermont fantasy you have ever had. And the best part is, it's all real.

Festivals

If you're planning to be in Woodstock for a sleigh ride and a visit to Gillingham's, you might as well come during *Woodstock's Winter Wassail Weekend* (http://www.woodstockvt.com/wassail.php). The highlight of the weekend is the Wassail Parade through the center of town. Troops of bands and carolers create a happy Christmas experience. There is a reading of A Child's Christmas in Wales at noon at the Norman Williams Library with hot cocoa and lots of homemade treats. It's a busy weekend.

Christmas at the Farm is an annual event at the nearby *Billings Farm and Museum* (www.billingsfarm.org; 802-457-235 5; 69 Old River Road, Woodstock, VT 05091). This is a working dairy farm where you can see cheese making and milking up close just as it has been happening for hundreds of years at family farms all over Vermont. Pretty much everyone leaves with a milk mustache and a bunch of new memories.

Christmas in Weston is a top-notch Christmas event (for information on visiting Weston go to www.weston-vermont.com). It includes a visit from Santa at The Vermont Country Store (see Country Stores, above), worth a visit for the famous old-fashioned candy counter alone. But during the season, Weston also has a live puppet show, a reading of Dickens's *A Christmas Carol* at the Old Parish Church, caroling in the Green, and a tree-lighting ceremony at dusk. Homemade fudge, bags of hot roasted chestnuts, sugarplums, and every Christmas treat you can dream of are always on hand. There is something about coming together with a bunch of strangers in woolen mittens and scarves, singing "Hark! The Herald Angels Sing" that would give even the scroogiest Scrooge a little Christmas spirit.

Bookstores (because bookstores are always a destination when we travel . . .)

New England has a rich history of booksellers, and *Northshire Bookstore* (www.northshire.com; 802-362-2200; 4869 Main St., Manchester Center, VT 05255) is one of the best, not just in the region but in the nation. This independent bookseller in Manchester, Vermont, is known for great local events and a thoughtful selection. The children's store all by itself is a good place to while away an afternoon. You'll find gifts, toys, and even a clothing line here. But this is not just a store filled with tchotchkes. This is a real bookstore. The buyers understand readers, and as a fiction reader who pays attention to publisher lists and reviews, I am always surprised by the great titles in their collection that I know I would never have found anywhere else. Online shopping may be great for shoes, but there is nothing like a real bookseller to draw your eye and your heart to a title. Many of my snowy weekends have been enriched by a trip to the Northshire.

Their Christmas gift selection is brilliant. You can find books for kids or foodies, travel enthusiasts or fiction lovers. The booksellers here are smart and well informed. Even better, they are good listeners. With just a few sentences from you about your intended recipient, their recommendations will be surprisingly thoughtful. Plus, they have a great café, the *Spiral Press Cafe* (www.spiralpresscafe.com). Great coffee, soups, and sandwiches in a cheerful, convivial space. While the kids choose their books and games you can have a really good cappuccino that will beat any chain coffee you have ever tasted. Winter is long up here. And I couldn't live in the North Country without this bookstore and these good people.

Ornaments

If you want to take home a lovely Christmasy souvenir or your own special ornament, there is no better place than *Magic Sleigh of*

Manchester (802-362-2197; 4960 Main St., Manchester Center, VT 05255). Owner Stephen Metcalf is coming up on his thirtieth Christmas season here and he can talk ornaments with the best of them. I think he must pipe the scent of Christmas nostalgia right into the shop's air, because every time I stop in I am walloped by all those tender feelings of Christmas past and the sweet anticipation of Christmas yet to come. The selection is exquisite. Tell him I sent you.

Resorts

Sticking close to home, there is the *Equinox Resort and Spa* (www.equinoxresort.com; 800-362-4747; 3567 Main St. Rte 7A, Manchester Village, VT 05254) in Manchester. Their Falcon Bar, serving cheese and chocolate, is the perfect place to spend a late afternoon as you regroup around the fireplace for supper. There are big colonial fireplaces everywhere here, and cheerful guys in flannel who keep the logs coming. They offer a Landrover driving school, falconry, snowshoeing, and cross-country skiing. And there's that spa. That big generous fireplace with the soft music is a perfect place to read, while you wait for your delicious massage or manicure.

After your morning sleigh ride or cross-country snow shoe down by the icy pond at the Equinox, you are going to be hungry. If I were you, I'd head over to Bonnie's at *Up For*

Breakfast (802-362-4204; 4935 Main St., Manchester, VT 05255). You might find a peppery brisket hash with poached eggs, or a local venison sausage with a blueberry sauce on the side. The Lignonberry Pain Purdu is a must-taste. Bonnie's list of specials are all local and always creative. Her buttermilk blueberry pancakes are as good as my grandma's were and that's saying something. I think Bonnie's restaurant is not just the best breakfast place in the area, but one of the best restaurants in Vermont.

Restaurants

But now we are talking food. And the very best restaurant in Vermont for my money has to be *The Downtown Grocery* in Ludlow (www .thedowntowngrocery.com; 802- 228-7566; 41 S. Depot St., Ludlow, VT 05149). Vermont is rich with choice, so this is the best in a field of great. Chef Rogan Lechthaler and his Mississippi-born wife, Abby Lechthaler, are cooking up New England specialties with a southern twist.

Imagine a braised Vermont pork belly with an apricot almond dulce. How about house-made tagliatelle with locally foraged mushrooms and a creamy white wine and garlic sauce? The local free-range fried chicken and grits with a rhubarb reduction practically made me swoon. Specialty cocktails—like the famed Vermont Mud Season (I think I can say "famed" if I want to) with Whis-

tlePig Rye, simple syrup, apple cider vinegar, and bitters—are delicious and well balanced. Chef Rogan cures his own meats and offers enticing charcuterie. Everything comes with homemade bread and biscuits. By the end of the meal, you will get the silly giggles when you hear about the desserts. Do not neglect dessert. The Vermont maple crème brulee is a favorite, but so is the local cheddar ice cream and the chocolate soufflé with a side of ice cream made from the Long Trail Brewery's stout.

We celebrate Christmas Eve here. And with the twinkly white lights, candles, white birch, and winterberries nestled against bottles of pink champagne, no place feels more like Christmas to me than this does. Abby runs the front of the house like it was supper on her back porch. Everyone feels welcome and happy, and her warm, exuberant attention is captivating.

Dogsledding!

Dogsledding is one of the most fun ways I know of moving through space and time and Vermont offers a bunch of choices. There is *Eden Dogsledding Adventures* up near Stowe (www.edendogsledding.com; 802-635-9070; 1390 Square Rd., Eden Mills, VT 05653), *Braeburn Siberians* in the Upper Valley (www.braeburnsiberians.com; 802-738-8337; PO Box 55, Windsor, VT 05089-0055), and *Husky Works Mushing Company* near Grafton (www.huskyworks.com; 5189 Rte. 100, West Wardsboro, VT 05360). These are ethical dog lovers who will wow you with their expert working teams. These dogs live for this work, and pretty soon so will you.

Skiing!

Lots of people think of snow and their first thought is of skis and snowboards. I am not that person. I am the one keeping the fire going and the cocoa hot, but I live in a family of boarders, so I know a lot about the best bets for Vermont skiing.

Stratton Mountain Resort (www.stratton.com; 1-800-787-2886; 5 Village Lodge Rd., Stratton Mountain, VT 05155) is a ski village with great trails, lodges, condos, a superior terrain park, horseback riding, snowshoeing, and a bunch of cute shops and restaurants for in between. Stratton offers high-end skiing with the services to match.

Okemo Mountain Resort in Ludlow (www.okemo.com; 1-800-786-5366; 77 Okemo Ridge Rd., Ludlow, VT 05149) is a family-friendly, laid-back ski experience. You can bring your three-year-old or your ninety-year-old grandma and everyone will be happy. The only heated chairlift in the Northeast is a big draw, as is the slope-side lodging. Okemo boasts two ski villages, Jackson Gore and Okemo Base Lodge, right in the middle of a real New England town. Okemo is gigantic, but somehow still a cozy experience. As a bonus, it's close to The Downtown Grocery.

Of course, you can't talk about skiing in Vermont without mentioning *Stowe Mountain Resort* (www.stowe.com; 802-253-3000 or 1-888-253-4849; 5781 Mountain Rd., Stowe, VT 05672). Stowe Mountain Lodge is perhaps the best known of the Vermont ski lodges. Mount Mansfield is Vermont's highest peak at 4,395 feet, and as a multidimensional activity destination, Stowe delivers. With more than fifty restaurants, lots of cozy B&Bs, high-end lodges, and spas, Stowe is a destination unto itself.

Fifteen minutes from Manchester, *Bromley Mountain Resort* (www.bromley.com; 802-824-5522 or 1-866-856-2201; 3984 Vermont Rte. 11, Peru, VT 05152) is a boutique family ski operation. Voted Best New England Kids Skiing year after year, Bromley knows its place in the world, and they don't mess it up by getting all fancy-pants. With a terrific southern exposure, Bromley is the Sun Mountain in Vermont. To kids the mountains look huge, and to parents they look just the right size, with slopes that funnel the whole family back to the centralized base and a lodge with good hearty food. There are always fun kid-centered activities, and the staff is knowledgeable, friendly, and warm. Bromley is where the locals take their own kids.

And of course, there's *Smugglers' Notch* (www.smuggs.com; 802-332-6841 or 1-800-419-4615; 4323 Vermont Rte. 108 South, Smugglers' Notch, VT 05464). Families come for fireworks, bonfires, and winter games like ice carving, ornament making, roasted marshmallow-treat contests, and sled building. You can come out and play broom ball on the ice or go tube sliding on Sir Henry's Hill. Serving up thirty-six flavors of hot cocoa, "Smuggs" is as good a place as any to find that Christmas feeling. Live music every day, plus plenty of après parties, makes Smugglers' Notch a favorite of locals and tourists alike.

New England Flavors: Online Retailers

The next best thing to being here . . .

Brockton Spice Company (www.brockton spice.com; 508-588-5932). Home of the original Ranch Hands Hearty Steak Seasoning (also known in our house as Peltier's Rub).

Consider Bardwell Farm (www.consider bardwellfarm.com; 802-645-9928) makes goat cheese just up the road from us, in West Pawlet. Angela Miller has brought this farm to life with her award-winning cheeses. The Dorset is a runny Taleggio that is just as good as any I ate in Tuscany. And the flavorful Rupert melts spectacularly in my mac 'n' cheese just like Gruyère. Her goats live happy, well-tended lives in the rolling mountains of Vermont.

Harlow's Sugar House (https://vermont sugar.com/maplesyrup.htm; 802-387-5852).

Straight from the tree. This syrup will make your blueberry pancakes taste like nature intended.

Hillside Lane Farm (www.hillsidelane; 802-728-0070) makes fruit-infused maple syrups like blueberry and apple. You think you know what fruit and maple syrup taste like, and then you taste this. I use the blueberry maple as a glaze on roasted chicken, and with some fresh blueberries strewn across the plate I look like a master chef. This stuff makes every cook look smarter. Some years they produce something called ample cream. It's more like butter and it is a table spread without compare. Serve it on muffins, scones, or even just toast. It is subtle and sexy.

Lake Champlain Chocolates (www.lake champlainchocolates.com; 1-800-465-5909) has great hot cocoa. For those nights when you want someone else to make it, order theirs. The Spicy Aztec is almost as good as mine.

Mother Myrick's Confectionery (www .mothermyricks.com; 1-888-669-7425). The best Vermont Buttercrunch in the whole world. Their Lemon Lulu cake is pretty special too.

Northshire Bookstore (www.northshire .com; 1-800-437-3700). 'Cause your brain needs candy too!

Small Batch Granola (www.smallbatchgra nola.com; 802-367-1054). Lindsay Martin is the Vermont chef who started this company. The granola is better than anything served at the most famous luxury hotels in the world. You serve this and you will feel like you are on vaca-tion every day. She makes a chocolate bark that is so divine, you will forget there is something healthy in your hands. It all tastes too decadent to be good for you!

The Vermont Country Store (www.ver montcountrystore.com; 1-800-547-7849). The salty licorice is just the way you remember it and, best of all, only a few people like us really love it so you won't have to share!

West River Creamery (www.westriver creamery.com; 802-824-6900). Every week I go to the Dorset Farmer's market just to find my pal Jane, who together with her husband, Charlie Parant, own the West River Creamery. I would make a detour on any New England vacation to eat this cheese. And now you can have it deliv-ered right to your door. Try the Glebe Moun-tain Swiss, which tastes nutty and fresh, or the Londonderry Reserve, a traditional clothbound English cheddar with tang.

Acknowledgments

Thanks to Todd Porter, my first editor, who has been making everything better around here for some twenty years. Thanks to my intrepid agent, Rosalie Siegel, who is now also my dear friend. Natalie Stultz took gorgeous photos and Sarah Hibler made everything prettier than we ever would have managed on our own. I had no idea how hard it would be to take one damn pretty picture of a cheese soufflé.

And thanks to everyone at Norton. They make smart beautiful books and I have been lucky to have them.

Most of all, thanks to my family John, Benjamin, Hannah, and Eli. This time, they even helped me throw a Christmas party in February so we could make this goofy deadline. And on that day, we had the kind of big family mishap that would have brought down a lesser group. These stalwart people I am related to coped with police, lawyers, firefighters, ambulances, and ER doctors. Somehow we still managed to throw an elegant dinner party for fifty, complete with caterers, cameras, lights, photographers, and friends from all over the country. It was pretty ridiculous. I have never loved any of them more.

Mousse, Chestnut, 55
movie night treats
    Maple Bacon Popcorn, 142–43
    Maple Fennel Sausage and Cheddar
        Meatballs, 147
    Pea Garlic Mascarpone Galette,
        148–49
    Prosciutto Fig Mascarpone Flatbread,
        144–46
Mud Season, 92
mushrooms, in Coq au Vin, 24
Mustard Champagne Vinegar, Warm, 26

N

nuts
    in Club Night Apricot Horns, 56–58
    Grandma Rimarchik's Slovak Nut Roll,
        208–9
    See also pecans; pistachio nuts; walnuts

O

Olive Oil Ice Cream, 109
Onion Bacon Tart, 178–79
Onion Pistachio and Lemon Winter
    Greens, Grilled, 258–59
Oysters with Homemade Tartar Sauce,
    Fried, 174–75
Oysters with Strawberry Mignonette,
    204–5

P

pancetta
    in Roasted Balsamic Brussels Sprouts,
        35
    Sage Pancetta Tagliatelle, 234–35
Panna Cotta, Buttermilk, 116
party foods
    Aunt Loraine's Brady Bunch Cheese
        Ball, 170–71
    Beef Tenderloin Sandwiches with
        Balsamic Onions and Gorgonzola
        Sauce, 160
    Candied Bacon-Wrapped Water Chest-
        nuts, 172–73
    Coffee Cream Puffs, 166–67
    Fried Oysters with Homemade Tartar
        Sauce, 174–75

Gorgonzola Sauce, 161
Homemade Mayonnaise, 177
Homemade Tartar Sauce, 176
Maple Fennel Sausage and Cheddar
    Meatballs, 147
Onion Bacon Tart, 178–79
Roquefort and Walnut Gougères, 163
Spicy Pecans, 168–69
Strawberry Salsa, 206
Todd and Natascha's Friend Amy's
    Christmas Hot Buttered Rum, 162
Yankee Deviled Eggs, 164–65
pasta and noodles
    Decadent Mac 'n' Cheese, 86–87
    Kugel, 243
    Sage Pancetta Tagliatelle, 234–35
    Tagliatelle, 232–33
Pea Garlic Mascarpone Galette, 148–49
peanut butter
    Peanut Butter Dog Treats, 127
    in Pupsicles, 131
pecans
    Aunt Loraine's Brady Bunch Cheese
        Ball, 170–71
    Grandma Rimarchik's Slovak Nut Roll,
        208–9
    John's Grandmother's Roszke Cookies,
        50
    Maple Pecan Cookies, 60–61
    in Salted Caramel Turtles, 70–71
    Spicy Pecans, 168–69
pet treats. *See* dog treats
pies, fruit
    Crostata, 112–13
    Grandma Lorraine's Cherry Pie with
        Crunchy Crumb top, 114–15
pies and tarts, savory
    Onion Bacon Tart, 178–79
    Tomato Pie, 34
Pig Candy, 54
pistachio nuts, in Grilled Onion Pistachio
    and Lemon Winter Greens, 258–59
Popcorn, Maple Bacon, 142–43
pork
    Citrus Soy Pork Loin, 30–31
    in John's Famous Chili, 80–81
    Root Beer Pulled Pork, 88–89

See also bacon; ham; pancetta; pro-
    sciutto; sausage
potatoes
    Garlicky Scalloped Potatoes, Luxuri-
        ous, 32
    Green Bean and Potato Soup, Grandma
        Rimarchik's Slovak, 93
    Guinness Beef Stew, 28–29
    Latkes, 195–96
    Loaded Mashed Potatoes, 106–7
    Potato Leek Soup, 82–83
Prosciutto Fig Mascarpone Flatbread,
    144–46
Prosciutto Gruyère Fennel Brioche,
    196–98
puddings
    Cardamom Tapioca Pudding, 84
    Corn Pudding, 108
Pupsicles, 131

R

Ramen, 260–61
rice, in Lemon Rice Soup, 257
Root Beer Pulled Pork, 88–89
Roquefort and Walnut Gougères, 163
rum, in Christmas Hot Buttered Rum, 162
Runny Bennie, 224
rye, in Mud Season, 92

S

Sage Pancetta Tagliatelle, 234–35
salads
    Grilled Onion Pistachio and Lemon
        Winter Greens, 258–59
Salsa, Strawberry, 206
Salted Caramel Turtles, 70–71
Sandwiches, Beef Tenderloin, with
    Balsamic Onions and Gorgonzola
    Sauce, 160
Santa's Shortbread, 66
sauces
    Caramel Sauce, 117
    Gorgonzola Sauce, 161
    Hollandaise, 225
    Homemade Mayonnaise, 177
    Homemade Tartar Sauce, 176
    Strawberry Salsa, 206